Beginner

+

Intermediate Guide to Wire Weaving

2-in-1 Wire Weaving Compendium

Table of Contents

Book 1: Wire Weaving for Beginners

Book 2: Intermediate Wire Weaving

omissions, or inaccuracies.

WIRE WEAVING FOR BEGINNERS

Make Your First Wire Jewelry Project and Learn Basic Wire Weaving Skills

INTRODUCTION

Wire weaving is a basic part of wire jewelry making. It is a vital technique and skill useful for projects that have to do with art, creativity, and wires. Patterns, curls, and directions are essential in wire weaving and must be properly understood to have the best of wire weaving works. Therefore, in the scope of this book, the integral knowledge needed for beginners in the art of wire weaving is provided in simple and clear words with no ambiguity at all. With total belief, this knowledge gives all and sundry the opportunity to make their first jewelry even without close supervision but just by the help of this book. This book covers basic weaves like the Snake Weave, Flame Stitch and other two-wire weaves. Also, various techniques such as coiling, wrapping, weaving, turtle necking to mention but a few, will be discussed. Three practical projects will be taught too with basic knowledge on how to make and install clasps, how to polish and wax the wires, how to splice and alongside incorporate beads into your designs. Helpful tips and links for better research and study are provided in the book with a chart on metric conversion. This book is amazingly perfect for beginners and can be used by experts too. It has been designed in a practical way; get the equipment needed and make your first wire weavings.

TOOLS

Here is a brief list of tools you will require:

1. Chain nose plier
2. Flat nose plier
3. Pointy flush cutter
4. Wires (of different types, lengths, diameters, sizes, and metals)
5. Clasps

DEFINITION OF TERMS

1. Weaving wire: Otherwise called warp wire/ adds-on wire. It is used to make the necessary movement when necessary. In most times it's very flexible and soft for wrapping around the base wire.

2. Base wire: This is the foundation of any wire works. It is very strong to withstand the rigorous movement of the warp wire. It is flexible but strong. It determines the shape and structure of the whole jewelry.

WEAVES AND TECHNIQUES

WEAVES

Two wire weaves

These two wire weaves are basic weaving styles and are also referred to as "wraparounds." This is to describe how the base wires are held together by wrapping weaving wires around them. Let's consider two weaves that employ the use of two wires.

Weave 1: The basic figure eight weave

For this weave, you will need two base wires (16, 18 or 20 gauge) with a particular length, which depends on how big your project is and a smaller gauge, though longer wire for wrapping.

Steps

1. Hold the two base wires, at the desired distance, in your left hand and wrap your weaving wire around the top base wire a

couple of times using your right hand. This is to attach your weaving wire to the base wire and give it a firm hold.

2. Wrap around each consecutively. I am going up and around the first base wire, down and between the two base wires then up, over and around the second base wire likewise.

This weave should produce a shape that looks like figure Eight around the bare wires. Repeat these steps until your desired length is reached.

Weave 2: Double Coils

This weave is similar to the basic figure eight weave. A slight change in the pattern is a double wrap around each of the two base wires before moving to the next. Just as indicated in the basic eight-figure weave, two base wires and a smaller weaving wire are needed.

Steps

1. Hold the two base wires at the desired
    distance in your left hand and wrap your
    weaving wire around the top base wire a
    couple of times using your right hand. This
    is to attach your weaving wire to the base
    wire and give it a firm hold.
2. Now wrap your weaving wire on the top
    base wire two times and then move between
    the two base wires to wrap the other base
    wire twice too.

Note that

1. The upper end of the base wires far above
    your right hand should be left open to allow
    you to weave between and around the wires
    comfortably.
2. To get good tension, pull the weave wire
    closely around the warp/base wire to form
    fine lines and for the weaving wires to really
    take the shape of the base wires.

3. After repeating the patterns, directions and
    flow couple of times, scoot them together if
    you find any weird space using your finger
    or nails. Do not use a tool to do this because
    you can knick up the wire.

4. Be careful not just to pull the weave wire
    around the base wire, leave it loose and try
    to tug, tug and tug until it tightens. This is
    because you are most likely going to get a
    kink or it will leave it with a lot of slack that
    will alter the weave. Instead, bring the wire
    all the way around the wire to which you
    want it on. All the way around, between and
    closely. Make sure that you are placing it
    where it is really ought to be craftily while
    bending it to the expected position.

5. For practice, improvise by using slightly
    thick copper wires for the base and any soft
    wire or copper too for weaving.

6. The number of wraps around each base wire
    is not limited to just one or two. A
    consistent number of your choice in one

design can be employed. Creativity is highly permitted though it must be done in symmetry, so it makes sense.

SNAKE WEAVE

The snake weave is a three wire weave that employs the use of three base wires of about 1 millimeter each and a weaving wire of any length. It is advisable to start with three feet for your weaving wire; this is because it is hard to weave when it's more than that. You can add more when you run out. This technique that involves ending a wire and adding another (splicing) is also discussed later in this book.

Steps

1. Attach the weaving wire to one of the base wires. Place another of the base wire, just above the first one and on top of the weaving wire. Then wrap around both wires twice just as if you have one base wire and

return to the position below the two base wires.

2. Now bring the third base wire and lay it above the rest of the base wires and on top of the weaving wire.

3. Pull the weaving wire from behind the new base wire upwards and in between the first two base wires.

   If you take the two wires and wrap both at the same time, there will be complete overlap of the wires, and this would not be able to get your weave wired up and coiled into the next direction.

4. Now wrap around the bottom two base wires twice again. Then push them all the way down with your fingers or nails gently.

5. Repeat these steps over and over till you have perfected the weave style or have met the expected length.

FLAME STITCH

This flame stitch looks like a weave with two sections looking different but are actually the same pattern of the basic weave. The only difference is that at the start of the weave, the weaves are tightly packed and barely spaced whereas the other section is well and nicely spaced with equal intervals and spaces. For this weave style, you will need five(5) base wires of about 1 mm and 18 gauge each and a length of 0.4mm round wire of about 26 gauge.

Steps

The closely packed section comes first

1. Grab one of your base wires and attach your weaving wire against the base wire just by wrapping a couple of times. Push the curls neatly together.

2. Add another base wire to expand the weave by placing it above the previous base wire and make the weaving wire come out between the two at the back. Then bring the

base wire around the bottom base wire then over against both of the base wires towards the back.

3. Add another base wire (the third one as at now). This wire will be on the top of the other base wires horizontally. The weaving wire is coming out from between the top two base wires (i.e., between the 2nd and 3rd; the newly added base wire).

4. Move the weaving wire between the two that you just wrapped (i.e., between the 1st and 2nd base wires). Push this all down and keep the distance and closeness constant. Then go all the way over the top two base wires and wrap around them.

5. After this, allow the weaving wire to go all the way down through the third base wire and over the two at the bottom (The same that were wrapped together at first). Allow the weaving wire to go down between the top two base wires.

6. The next base wire is placed, unlike the former ones, below the others and on top of the weaving wire. The weaving wire then goes all the way behind the base wires and over the top two bottom base wires so that the new wire is included. Now the weaving wire is between the 2nd and 3rd bottom base wires at the back.

7. The fifth and last base wire is now added at the bottom below all others, like the recent former base wire. The weaving wire comes behind all the base wires from the 2nd bottom base wire and over the top of the bottom two base wires, so the new one is included. Always remember to push the wavy pattern all the way down to keep it close and neat. The weaving wire is now between the now 2nd and 3rd base wires

8. From behind the 3rd out of the five base wires, come in between the two you just wrapped up (i.e., between the 1st and 2nd bottom base wires), to return to the middle

base wires in order to perform the same wavy weaves on the other side. Move the weaving wire upward over the next two base wires and down between the 3rd and 4th base wires. From behind, go between the two base wires you just wrapped together.

9. Go over the next two base wires (i.e., the 4th and 5th), then move down behind three base wires going back to the middle base wire. Here the weaving wire is between the 2nd and 3rd base wires.

10. Once more, move over the two base wires going upwards and down between the 4th and 5th base wires.

11. Again, move the weaving wire up over the next two base wires so that the weaving wire is between the 3rd and 4th base wires and down behind the 4th base wire. You can then move the weaving wire up between the two you just wrapped (i.e., the weaving wire will be found between the 3rd and 4th base wires).

12. From the current location of the weaving wire, move down again under all the base wires and over the top of the two at the bottom, so it is stationed in between the 2nd and 3rd base wires, and between the two you just wrapped. After that, move over the next two including the middle base wire, so your weaving wire is between the 3rd and 4th base wire.

The spaced section of the flame stitch is just as indicated for the first section but rather more spaced.

Steps

1. After you must have repeated the patterns of the first section explained above severally, finish your curl and allow the weaving wire to be just behind the middle base wire; having two at the top and three below. So the weaving wire is between the 3rd and 4th base wire.

2. Wrap the weaving wire around the middle base wire a couple of times, this is dependent on you and how far apart you want them to be. For example, use three wraps.

3. The weaving wire should be just between and below the 3rd and 4th base wire. The same pattern as explained in the first section is what you do here too, but the spacing (that is, the three wraps around the middle base wire at intervals) is what makes the difference.

4. The wire comes from behind the middle wire, and over the next two wires and up between the two you just wrapped. It then goes over the top of the next two base wires, down behind them and again up below the middle wire.

5. Before you go to the next side, wrap around the middle base wire three times, as proposed and just as you started. Then move down over the next two base wires

which are above the middle base wire. This places the weaving wire in between the 3rd and 4th base wires, down behind and all the way over the top of the bottom two.

6. Finally, come up between the two base wires you just wrapped and push it down and over the next two base wires just above the middle wire. Also, put it between the 3rd and 4th base wires and go through the spacing again(the three wraps around the middle base wire)

Lastly, repeat the weaves until your desired length is attained.

TECHNIQUES

COILING

In wire weaving and jewelry making, coiling is a basic and essential technique that should be learned and incorporated. Coiling is an easy wire working technique and would be explicitly explained in this section. Coiling involves using a weaving wire around a base wire in the form of a helix. It is advised that you practice this wire weaving technique with brass or copper wire before you get to perfection.

For this technique you'll need:

5 inches length of 16 gauge base wire

2 feet of 18 gauge weaving/wrapping wire

Ruler or Tape rule

Marker

Chain/flat nose plier

Pointy flush cutter

Steps

1. Using the Pointy flush cutter, cut 5 inches length of 16 gauge wire for your base wire and 2 feet length of 18 gauge wire for your weaving wire after marking these lengths using your ruler. Mark out, at both ends, 1inch on your 5 inches base wire using your marker.

2. Use your flat nose plier to grasp the end of the weaving wire and bend it to about 45 degrees towards yourself. This serves as a tail that gives the weaving wire a better grip for coiling.

3. Using your left (non-dominant) hand, hold the tail end of the wire between your index finger and your thumb and slide the base wire into the bent space of the weaving wire.

4. Starting from the 1inch marked point on your base wire, use your plier to squeeze gently the bent weaving wire against the base wire. Push outwards and downwards

the weaving wire to begin the coils around the base wire.

5. Keep the coils running around the base wire repeatedly till you have reached the other 1inch mark. Use your Pointy flush cutter to cut the excess weaving wire away. To tidy things up, use your chain nose plier to tuck each end of the weaving wire in.

And you're done! Your coiled wire is ready.

WRAPPING

In the auspices of expounding and learning wire weaving skill, wrapping is a technique that requires using wire. It teaches how to wrap around a loop. This loop helps you attach this piece with other wire loops to make a necklace and/or bracelet.

For this technique, you will need:

Just a wire; the base wire

Round nose pliers

Pointy flush Cutters

Ruler

Steps

1. The very first thing to do is to measure and cut the wire (of your desired length, let's say 6inches) for usage. Make sure it is straight and not rumpled.

2. Using your dominant hand, take up your plier, and make a 90degree bend at a marked point of 2.5 inches from the end of the wire. Thereafter, twist the bent wire backward using your round nose plier, the tail should be hanging down!

3. Make sure to hold your round nose plier in your dominant hand with the bent wire pointing towards you from between the pliers. You can now bend the end of the short wire back using the thumb of your nondominant hand. And with plier, bend the shorter end of the wire around the other end.

4. Now remove the plier from the semi-circle loop you just made, reinsert the plier and twist the loop, reassembling it to form a perfect circle.

5. Hold onto the loop gently using your plier to prevent plier marks on it. Using your fingers, wrap the end of the wire around the stem of the loop tightly.

6. With about three to four rounds around the loop, you have made a great example of the wrapping technique. Cut out, cautiously, the excess short wire using your pointy flush cutter and avoid a sharp edge.

SPLICING

Splicing is a very simple technique basically created through a loop and at least three wires. Very many workers employ splicing, but it is basic and unique to wire works. The goal is to create a kind of hair-plaited look; thus, the need to have three wires crossed together which are held at the loop end with a plier. It is advisable to use soft and flexible wire for a beginner alongside handkerchief to hold the wires to avoid bruise. Most importantly, splicing is used in joining wires together; a process no wire weaving expert could elude while creating jewelry.

Splicing requires the following equipment:

6" to 3" Wires cut; the base and working

Round nose pliers

Chain nose pliers

A wire gauge

Steps

1. The first thing to do is to gauge how long you want the wire to be which should be based on the kind of jewelry to be made.
2. Then, pick the wires and make a cut of 2 and half of 16 or 18-inch gauge of the wires. Pick up your round nose pliers, make a loop and use it to hold the loop relative tight. You have to be careful with the manner the wire will be

turning around the plier, hold it firmly and avoid movement whatsoever.

3. After you have got stability, push the wire at the extreme towards the loop you are holding and coil –the coiling process was the first technique to be explained, revise it, if need be.

4. After the coil, move the pliers to it and push the working wire (the major wire you are using to the coil) to make a continuous coil until you've gone round with enough.

5. At this point, hold the wires with your hand and remove the pliers to make a quick bend and continue with the coiling, make it halfway through.

6. With the bend, you have made a demarcation which will guide you. Use the round nose pliers to the grasp the wire in the about ¼ way along with the coil, then push the ends towards the jaw.

7. Then, you will need to make a finch end of the wires through the chain nose pliers. To do

this, make an upward but tiny bend at the tip end of the hook using the pliers.

8. Move the loop towards the jewelry and use the rubber mallet to hit it.

Make sure you repeat processes until the desired result is got. Alas, your splicing is very much ready!

GOOSENECK HOOK

This kind of technique of more or less like an addition to a primary design. This is because gooseneck hook is basically used in bracelet and necklace which are designed using other techniques. As important as starting jewelry is, finishing it up with gooseneck hook is one of the things any designer can't elude, even you. Gooseneck serves as connecting link with air in jewelry designing. Note that, this hook will add about a quarter inch to your length and thus proper considerations must be given to it.

Coming up with a good gooseneck hook technique, the following are the basic equipment

for a workable gooseneck hook:

Wires 16 to 18 gauge

Round nose pliers

Chain nose pliers

Hammer

Steps

1. Since it is more or less addition to works, the first thing to do is to create a loop using the sharp end of your pliers.
2. Hold tight the loop and push the tail end of the wire towards it, start making a coil.
3. With this, a new part must've been created, move the pliers from the loop to the new part and hold the wire for continuous coiling until it moves about the loop.
4. After creating the coil, you will need to create a bend using the round nose pliers and

continue with the wire movement around the coil in about halfway distance.

5. After enough coiling, use the more significant part of the round nose pliers hold the active wire and push it to the jaw. Make sure you observe about one-quarter distance away from the coil.

6. To the chain nose pliers, remember the round nose is still holding the wire, drag the wire till you get a tiny tip, make a bend and pinch it. Slip the hook now towards a piece of jewelry.

7. Lastly, depending on the wires used; 16 or 18 gauges; hit the hook slightly until a smooth is reached.

CRISS-CROSS FINISHED ENDS

This technique is like a finished cleaning means of keeping and tucking every end of the wires used in production. Of course when you create pieces of jewelry, many of the wires, both base and working, might be remaining at the tail end. These tail end will, in order to make the work neat, need to be kept –the process of maximizing this is crisscross finished ends. With this technique, tapping don the bracelet in order to create a loop for the clasp is done in a simple way. There are different sizes of wires to be used in this technique but start with 16 base alongside 8 and 9 add-on wires. You will need to get the 16 gauge as the base then pull the 8 gauge to the left end side while the 9 to the extreme left side crossed over the 8 gauge. With this first adjustment, all the wires are to be used as the base. These gauges aren't strictly used; you can choose to do it with another gauge but be sure every step meets the expected ends.

To make great crisscrossed ends, the following are what would be needed:

Wires in 16, 20, 8, 9, 15, etc. gauges

14 and 20 framing wires

Chain nose pliers

Round nose pliers

Nylon-jaw pliers

Steps

1. Based on the fact that you have created a crossed-wire, try to pick the 9 gauged wire and bend it towards the center of the base. Likewise, make the same kind of bend towards the center of the base wires 15 and 16 for 8 gauge wire.

2. When everything is intact, turn the work over and work from the other side of it. With this done, you will need to measure 38 in from the wires and trim.

3. Then, looping the wires to outside the 20 gauge base wire is the next thing to do. You could label the wires to avoid confusion, even though variation in sizes should be a hint.

4. The wires being outside, then insert, with equal spacing and varying colors, up to 60 beads on all the wires in the 20 gauge.

Again, you will need to do the steps from the beginning; bend, loop and trim wires outside the 20 gauge wire. Note that every wire trimmed must be held tight and make sure every end that meets at 20 gauge cross over one another.

5. Keep at piling up wires, trimming and crossing them too. You should notice the shape formed by the wires is a pyramid. Use the flat nose pliers to bend the framing wires to the center.

6. Then, make a cross over at the left side of your works. Make sure the 20 and 14 gauged wires are wrapped together –use the wrapping technique here; revisit if need be.

7. You are coming to the conclusion now. Trim the ends and maintain the balance of the pyramid by using the nylon-jaw pliers. Let everything be held tightly and wrap all the top (14) and bottom (20)

framing wires. Hold every scattering ends, trim them when necessary.

The work is read. Do make sure every step that didn't give the desired output should be repeated.

SPIRALS

Spirals are done in a special way with the aim of achieving curly-look designs. It is explicitly done with other techniques in order to make unique effects on the wiring works. It creates a distinctive look around the jewelry. Meanwhile, spirals can be used to make any kind of wire weaving works such as pendants, bracelets, necklaces, and lots more. Note that whatever jewelries you want to create, the steps and equipment are given, here, remain the basic for them.

Spirals construction require the following equipment:

Wires of 16" inch

Wire cutter

Round nose pliers

Ruler

Permanent marker

Hammer

Steel bench

File or knife sharpening stone

Steps

1. To start spirals, make from the 16 gauge wire a 3" long cut from all the wires you will be using

2. Then, use your permanent marker to make demarcation of ¼ cm and file one tip end of the wire

3. With this, create a loop around the measurement using the round nose pliers.

4. Then, hold the loop firmly, either with your hand or chain nose pliers, thrust your index finger or make coils.

5. As you are making progress in coiling, move the position of the pliers from where you put it, either right or left, keep the coil going and push the chain nose downwards.

6. At the lower part of the coil, make a wrap at the end. This is the way you will be making the spiral until you get the length needed for your job.

Keep at this motion; removing and repositioning of the chain nose pliers, making coils and adding wrap at every end.

TURTLENECKING

This is a very fancy-oriented weaving decoration. Mostly likely with small and or other types of beads attached on the woven and coiling weaving, turtle necking is done to strengthen and prove the potency of the beads on the works. Basically, all that you are doing is simply wrapping ½ of the beads through the 24" on the working wire. In this technique, you will need to copper round the beads with its shimmer.

For a successful turtle necking, you will use the following basically:

Wires that is 24 gauge –a base and add-on

Wire cutter

Beads

T-pin

Thread

Holder

Round nose pliers

Steps

1. Pick up the adds-on and base wires. Take the woven wire, and use the T-pin to make a hole through it until you have variation in the wires (one longer than the other). You will need to wriggle the thrust very well, be careful though.

2. Then, continue this kind of thrust and intersection on all the points you want to turtle neck.

3. Pick your 24 gauge adds-on wire and make a cut of about 3 inches on it.

4. Pick the thread and thrust it through the loop created by the T-pin. Make sure you wrap the wire end twice and cut or trim the tips.

5. After then, through the right side beside the base wires, bring the add-on wires from the back end and attach a bead to it. Make sure when you're pushing the wires that they are towards the weave created.

6. You will need to balance the position of the wires, so pick the adds-on wire in between the base wire and make sure it is at the center. To ensure everything is tight, pull the base and add-on wires.

7. Like you did with bring the adds-on wire to the center through the base wires from the back, bring the wire again near the beads and make sure every space is guided firmly.

8. When you have got the adds-on wires close to the beads, wrap them about two hundred and twelve times around the beads and make sure you pull the wire tight through the beads.

9. Do you remember that your T-pin that started the work is right there? Fine, bring the wire through the same direction you started with. Be extremely careful as the wire will want to shrink and rip off even from the loop; control this by hold from the loop your wires with holder, perhaps wires.

10. Lastly, remove the holder from the loop, straight the wires smoothly with round nose pliers and your work is ready.

Note that handling the wires firmly, especially the base wires, with your steady hand and move the adds-on wires with the weak one as this process could be a bit tedious without proper monitoring. For a start, ensure you repeat the process whenever you get stocked or move without getting the desired goals. You can start off, after the first step, to use the holder in order to have everything intact to avoid any form of frustrations through repeated getting of undesired and deserved results. Be extremely careful but creative.

PROJECTS

WOVEN LINK NECKLACE

To work out a project, be prepared to 'waste' materials and repeat the same thing at different times. The heart of this work is based on the first half of the Flame Stitch weave. These wire works are one of the most basic that used the techniques discussed. This work is a necklace weaved together. It is gorgeous and adjustable. This necklace is adjoined with turquoise seed beads. With a spiral technique, individual woven links are joined together. You must give yourself to much practice till the uphill pattern is formed. You must be prepared to start the work and finish on the spot, at least as a beginner.

Techniques for the woven link necklace are:

Weaving

Wrapping

Spiral

Goose necking

Cutting of wires

Therefore, revise the technique at a glance and do as instructed. You have to inculcate neatness in your work from the beginning.

To do this beginner project, you will need the following materials:

32 in. 18-gauge dead soft copper wire

80 in. 20-gauge dead soft copper wire

15 ft. 24-gauge dead-soft copper wire

11 to 60 Turquoise seed beads

Chain nose pliers

Flush cutter

The step by step guide, to be followed strictly:

Step 1

You will need to create the base of woven first. For the base wire of the woven link, pick the 20 gauge wire and cut four, of 4-inches, pieces of 20-gauge wire.

Step 2

Then for the weaving, cut a 3-ft. piece of 24-gauge wire to be used straightened before weaving, though.

Step 3

Complete the Uphill Wire Preparation, double wrap for the Flame Stitch with four base wires.

Step 4

Afterward, start with the first base wire by bringing the weaving wire straight down and working on the uphill portion of the Flame Stitch.

Step 5

Then double wrap the wires at this point. Make sure everything is intact and not loosened.

Step 6

Gradually, as you reach the top of each hill, move downwards, just behind the current place you are, with the weaving wire, and go directly into the uphill weave on the base wire again.

Step 7

Repeat the weave until you have woven 2 inches. You must be using the ruler at this point to monitor the progress of the weave.

Step 8

You will need to center the weave, now, pull each base wire outward with chain nose pliers. Because of the way you have been weaving, notice that the ends of the wires are not equal and trim the ends so you have one-quarter inches of wire on every side.

Step 9

Using three-step pliers, grasp all four wires on end at the same time and roll them inward for medium-sized loops.

Step 10

Leave the loops open so you can slide the connector in place later. Do this on both ends to finish your first woven link.

Step 11

The work is almost ready, and you have just laid a good foundation for your work. For the complete work, you will need more than two wovens. Therefore to get up to five woven links, repeat steps six and seven. Put them in another place; you will know where to join them later.

Step 12

Because you have five woven links, make five Spiral Connectors, a Gooseneck Hook, and a tip for your extension chain.

Step 13

You must have got the last shape of the work. With the spiral connectors connect together all the pieces from the beginning. Likewise, the loops should be connected to the ends of the woven links. Join all five of the woven links as well.

Step 14

Pick the chain nose pliers and tighten each loop around the spiral connector.

In order to let the necklace fit, customize by laying it down and massage with the mallet. Be careful not break beads sandwiched therein.

Your necklace is ready, flaunt it to impress people. CHUCKLES!

WOVEN EARRINGS

To make a stunning look, for a lady, put on a pair of simple but sophisticating earrings. These earrings are made with and display a pair of vibrant stones. Among all things to do first, you must first weave, in a single wrap, the base wire in order to frame up your Flame Stich's patterns. This weave must be four in number for energetic downhill patterns.

The techniques to employ for this project include:
Weaving
Wrapping
Crisscross

The materials are:
Pair of decorative earring
32 in. 20-gauge dead-soft sterling-silver wire
Chain nose pliers
20 in. 26-gauge dead-soft sterling-silver wire
Flame stitch
4 ft. 24-gauge dead-soft sterling-silver wire
2 to 3mm round sterling silver beads

2 to 10x15mm amethyst cabochons

Cutter

Ruler

The step by-step-guide:

Follow the steps below strictly and observe the change you make at every point:

Step 1 (cutting)

You're starting with your 20 gauge wire for the base. On the wire, cut four 4-in. pieces and make sure you check whether their sizes are equal. Drop this.

Pick your 24-gauge wire that will be used for waving and make a cut of 2-ft. pieces.

Step 2

Because you'll need to complete the uphill wire planning and arrangement, with your base wire (20-gauge), make a single wrap with all the four base wires. Drop this.

Step 3

Measure 1 inch of flame stitch. From the downhill to the uphill pattern making, weave alternately, the downhill to the uphill. To know whether you have completed a hill, weave one uphill and one downhill weaving pattern consecutively.

Step 4

You will make a full 14 hills that are one-inch long weave pattern. Make sure –through pulling every base wire using the chain nose pliers –every of your weave is center on the base wires.

Step 5

At this point, you'll have to make sure there is about 1½ in. of a weave on the sides; both base and working wires. Make sure the weaves are tightly held together to avoid scattering.

Step 6

Once you attained stability, pick up your stones. Then, make a U-shape, bend the weave that is close to the curve of one end of your stone. Note that the shape you've carved doesn't have to be perfect, but a little smaller than the stone itself. At the top, crisscross the base wires, alternating left and right.

Step 7

Back to the base wires, pull all the four wires downwards equally and placed within the same spacing.

Step 8

Then, with your index finger and thumb on the left, hold the sixth wire tightly and bend the first base wire over it like a crisscross. Total carefulness needs to be taken here as you pull the wires and cross them on one another –you must maintain the shape throughout. While you are moving around the stones, ensure that the grip on the sixth base wire isn't jeopardized. Do this again and again.

Step 9

After the moving of base wires, turn the weave to the

other side and trim the first base wire to about 3/8 inches.

Step 10

With the chain nose pliers, make a single and loose wrap of base wire one and six. Perhaps you label the wires for easy identification. Put the wire in their right proportion and don't let them stiff. Note that the best thing to do is to start with this loose wrapping and locking of each base because it makes the work easier and gives it the desired, don't forget to keep the shape all the time.

Step 11

It is time to insert the stone. Make sure the weave you have created is relatively small so that the stone will fit in very well –which is the bezel –trim the loops and tight them.

Step 12

That part is ready, and you will need to do the same thing for the other base wires to make sure the direction of movement is inward and held tight together during the wraps making.

Step 13

When you are done, at the top of everything, make a wrap and hold the intersected area with the chain nose. Make sure you trim the left side sixth base wire.

Put in a 3mm bead on the 6th base wire and make a double wrapped weave just above the bead while making a connection to the earring before the wrap is complete.

Using your pointy flush cutter, trim the wrap closely on the back.
Strap the stone into the bezel.

Cut a 10 inches piece of 26 gauge wire; this you will use to wrap the left side of the weave, towards the end. Wrap this wire around the weave about 5-6 times, then to the right, next to where the crisscross section begins. Trim the end close on the back.

Now crisscross the stone like you are lacing up your shoe using the 26 gauge wire. Go backward and forward five times. Wrap around the 6th base wire using the 26-gauge wire three times to the crisscross section so as to replicate the wrap made before. Trim the end closely and neatly on the back. Make the second earring to make a pair. Create a finish with liver of sulfur and buff.

DONUT BAIL PENDANT

This is very simple work and thus requires simple skill. Because of its end product, which is a whole donut bail pendant, there will be a preparative work prior to the main job. In other words, this project is a beginner one but combines simple preparatory works with the main one. The preparation is expedient because without it the foundation will not be made for the huge job. In the same vein, the main job needs a pendant so, make sure the size and type of the pendant are determined too. Make sure you follow the steps swiftly even as you read.

The following are techniques needed to finish the job:

Weaving

Downhill single Flame Stitch

Wrapping

These techniques are very basic and must have been acquired from the beginning of this book if otherwise, make sure you revise the section that deals with techniques.

Materials:

33 in. 20-gauge dead-soft copper wire

3½ ft. 24-gauge dead-soft copper wire

50mm gemstone donut

10mm large-hole copper bead

3mm bead

40 80 seed beads

Daisy spacer with large hole

Ruler

Chain nose pliers

Round nose pliers

The following are the things to get ready before going to the main work:

Step 1

Weave a bail for a donut-shaped stone with about a large 50mm jasper donut.

Step 2

Make sure that the weave is adjustable to fit any size

Step 3

Prepare the Downhill Single Flame Stitch technique for it would be needed at the woven section.

Step 4

You will need to learn if you have not mastered how to embellish with seed beads for a dash of color and texture.

To the main project now, make sure everything needed –the techniques, materials and the pre-working stages –is ready.

Then follow the step-by-step guide below:

Step 1

Making the base wire. For the base wire, pick a 20-

gauge wire and cut six pieces of it. Drop this.

Step 2

Then, pick the 24-guage wire and cut one piece of it for the weaving wire.

Step 3

At this stage, you will need to know how much wire needed for your base stone.

Step 4

Then, Wrap a cord or string through the stone.

Step 5

Make a mark for the overlap.

Step 6

Caution needs to be taken here make sure the measurement of this length is 2½ inches.

Step 7

To complete the overlapping, add 3 in. to that

measurement of the length of the base wires.

Step 8

Make a cut of six 5½ in. pieces of wire.

Step 9

Pick up the base wire #6 at the top of the Weave.

Step 10

You will need to string a 60 seed bead about 1 in. from the end of base wire 6.

Step 11

Make sure that this spacer bead makes room in the weave to add more beads later.

Step 12

Pick the weaving wire, now, place it to the right of the bead and on top of the base wire. Make sure the placement is 1 in. from the end.

Step 13

Then, at the center where both wires (base and weaving) overlapped, hold it with your left thumb and index finger.

Step 14

With everything held in the right place and proportion, wrap the weaving wire three times to the right of the bead.

Step 15

You want to prepare the base wires for weaving. Do this by doing the Downhill Wire Preparation.

Step 16

For this Downhill wire preparation, make a single Wrap.

Step 17

On base wire #1, at the bottom of the weave, string a spacer seed bead, and then complete the last wrap of the Downhill Wire Preparation.

Step 18

Remove the two spacer beads to the left and slide them back on base wires #1 and #6 to the right of the weave.

Step 19

Bring the weaving wire from behind up two base wires and go between base wires #4 and #5.

Step 20

Note that this must put you at the top of the hill as you bring the weaving wire up, over, and straight down the back, making the jump behind the weave so you can repeat the downhill pattern.

Step 21

Begin Downhill Flame Stitch Weave single wrap. At the bottom of every hill, at base wire #1, string a seed bead on base wires #1 and #6.

Step 22

You will continue with Downhill Flame Stitch Weave, stringing seed beads on base wires #1 and #6 as you go.

Step 23

Don't panic if your stitches don't want to stay in neat i.e., like in the diagonal lines because you could pinch them with chain nose pliers to make them line up.

Step 24

Now, continue the Downhill Flame Stitch Weave for the length you originally measured with the cord.

Step 25

When the weaving is completed, slide each wire out individually until the weave is centered.

Step 26

Then, wrap the weaving wire three times around base wire #6 and trim the end tightly on the back.

Step 27

You will need to push the weave into the hole of the stone and center the stone.

Step 28

With this, make a U-shaped bend to fit the stone very well. Now, remove the stone.

Step 29

You must have noticed that there are several ends that need to be finished.

Step 30

Because of this, make a 90-degree bend inward with base wires #1 and #6. They should cross each other inside the weave.

Step 31

At this stage, end base wires #2, #4, and #5 straight down on the inside of the weave, over the top of the two crossed wires. Make sure you trim all the three wires to about 3/8 in.

Step 32

With the round nose pliers, curl the ends of the three wires over the crossed wires to lock them in place.

Step 33

Trim the two crossed wires close, up against base wires #2 and #5.

Step 34

Repeat steps 9–11 on the other side of the weave. Put the donut back in.

Step 35

Then, with chain nose pliers, pinch the two #3 base wires that are standing straight up.

Step 36

This will bring the two sides in, right up against each other for the next step.

Step 37

Make a double wrap around one of the #3 base wires.

It doesn't matter which one, as long as it is tight.

Step 38

Trim the end and pinch it down.

Step 39

On the remaining base wire, string a spacer bead, a 10mm copper bead, and a 3mm bead.

Step 40

Make a Double-Wrapped Loop at the top of these beads. If you are adding a chain as you must have planned, connect the chain to the loop before you complete the wraps.

Your work is now ready. This is a very simple way of making stunning jewelry.

DOUBLE-CROSSED WOVEN BRACELET

This exceptionally beautiful bracelet has a large center focal bead. This project can be a little bit tricky because the woven bezel has two open ends, but you get better with practice.

Materials:
- 19 in. 14-gauge dead soft copper wire
- 7 ft. 20-gauge dead-soft copper wire
- 8 ft. 24-gauge dead-soft copper wire
- 20x25mm cabochon
- 18 80 seed beads

Materials for the Bezel:
- 3 ft. 20-gauge dead-soft copper wire
- 2 ft. 24-gauge dead-soft copper wire

Steps

1. To start with, measure 9 and a half inches piece of your 14 gauge wire and cut. You will need two of this for the outer frame

wires. Measure and cut eleven, 7 and a half inches of your 20 gauge wire, these are the base wires. Measure and cut two 3 and a half feet of your 24 gauge wire for the weaving wires. Get your tools in place, and work starts.

2. Pick the 14 gauge base wire, make a wraparound it three times using the end of the weaving wire. Make the wires firm by weaving a double wrap for the six base wires. For this project, the scale weave is employed. It is essential to identify the center wire. To do this, therefore, it becomes easier to identify when you pull out that center wire a little farther than all the other base wires.

3. Pick another new 14 gauge wire, wrap the weaving wire around it three times, do this till you complete the uphill wire preparation using the double wrap for seven base wires.

4. Place the first section above the second and using the top weaving wire, wrap twice around the 7th and 8th base wires. Now the two sections are joined, the snake weave can begin.

5. Starting with the bottom weaving wire, wrap twice around the 6th and 7th base wires. Note that the 7th base wire is the center wire. Continue the double snake weave for eight stitches. Here the weave starts to separate and a diamond-like shape is formed.

6. Pick the top weaving wire that is between the 7th and 8th base wires and weave the flame stitch weave upwards, making double wraps till the top. On the lower section, push the bottom waving wire down from behind and then pull up between the 4th and 5th base wires. Then wrap twice around the 5th and 6th base wires. Continue this downwards using

the flame stitch weave, making double wraps
till the bottom.

7. On the other upper half, weave four stitches
    of double wrap flame stitch downwards. On
    the lower half, weave upwards using the
    flame stitch. And wrap around the 6th and 7th
    base wires twice, with double wraps till the
    middle.

8. Just as you did when you were joining the
    two sections together before, bring the top
    weaving wire down to wrap 7th and 8th base
    wires twice. Complete the Double Snake
    Weave for 16 stitches. This is the foundation
    for the focal stone. Separate the weave as
    you did in step 5. Make the same diamond
    shape in the weave. When the two weaving
    wires come again together, weave double
    snake weave for eight stitches.

9. Repeat step 5 to separate both sections. Then
    wrap 3 times, the weaving wire around the

13th base wire. Trim each of the weaving wire close to the back and pinch downwards. Place the weave on the base wires and complete a crisscross finished end on each end of the bracelet. Be sure to start with one seed bead on the 12th base wire, to stay in place and make up for the odd number of the base wires.

10. On the end of the crisscross sections, make a double wrap loop. Thus part of the piece is finished.

Now! **The double-crossed bezel** is next.

Step 1

Measure and cut two 6inches pieces of 20gauge for the outside base wires. Measure from the 20-gauge wire eight pieces, 3inches each and cut them. Measure and cut two 12 inches of 24 gauge weaving wire.

Step 2

Weave the sides of the bezel. Using a single wrap, measure and cut four 3inches pieces of 24-gauge wire and one 6inches piece. Weave six hills using the flame stitch and single wraps. Once this is done, repeat the whole process while turning it 180 digress to make an identical piece that is a mirror image of the first bezel side.

Step 3

Push both pieces of the bezel into the side of the stone. Use the stone to mold the shape. Crisscross the base wires of each of the bezel piece. Pull the first two base wires down and over the opposite side so that they almost touch the woven part. This indicates where you should make the first loops on the crossed wires. Turn it around and do the same thing on the other side—crisscross the wires and pull the first two down

Step 4

Wrap the first two base wires on each side around

the opposite side with a loose loop, and this is to keep the open ends balanced so that the weaving come smooth and fitting. Do not tighten this yet, just wrapped around the edges to hold the bezel intact.

Step 5

With the first two base wires holding the shape, wrap the other base wires around the opposite sides, trim them about 3/8 in., and make a loose loop around the outside base wire. Try not to pull in on the outside base wire and keep the original shape established by the first two base wires.

Step 6

Wrap the ends of the other side as you did the first, taking care to maintain the shape of the bezel. On the back, tighten the loops by trimming them if they are too long and pinching them down. Keep checking the fit by putting the stone back in and molding the wire to the contour.

Step 7

Bend the two long base wires on either side of the bezel straight back at a 45-degree angle. Slide the two base wires inside the diamond pattern with the center wire between them. Do this on both sides. Use a T-pin to make room for the base wires if they don't want to go in there. Put the stone in the bezel and slide it up to the bracelet to secure it.

Step 8

On the back, bend the base wires to the side, go through the 5th base wire of the bezel, and pull it straight down. Don't tighten it yet; leave it a little loose. Do this to all four base wires, so they hold the bezel right up against the bracelet.

Step 9

As you make the loops, check to make sure the bezel is in the center of the bracelet. Tighten the loops underneath when you are sure the bezel is placed where you want it.

Trim the loops and pinch them down to tighten. Trim

the base wires and pinch them down.

To conclude,

Step 10

Make a gooseneck hook and attach it as a clasp to the end of the bracelet. Bend the bracelet to fit the hand you want to. Try it on!

Step 11

Create a finish with liver of sulfur and hand buff.

MAKING AND INSTALLING CLASPS

When ending a piece of jewelry, most notably, bracelet, necklace, etc., the clasp is what hold the two ends together. A clasp connects both ends of the piece, allowing you to open and close the piece when putting it on or taking it off while complimenting its beauty. There are quite a number of clasps designs, and this is also subject to creativity and innovation. Many types of clasps are available in the market for purchase, but you make yours. To mention but a few, we have the loop clasps, S-clasp, etc.

In this book, we will be considering how to make a few clasps and also how to install them.

1. **S-Clasp**

    Materials:

    Wire- two pieces of 20 gauge wire of 3cm each

    Round nose pliers

    Mandrel- pen (this is optional)

Steps

a. Measure and cut the stipulated amount of wire. Mark, using a marker, the 1/3 point of the wire both from ends and using a round nose plier, make a curve in the wire at each of this point to form an S shape.

b. With the tip of your round nose plier, make small loops at each ends facing outwards.

c. Now close one side tightly though cautiously. The open side serves as the clasps.

NOTE: To install this S-Clasp on a bracelet or necklace. Attach one side to one loop of the bracelet before closing it tightly. The other side will be left open, and this side gives ease of wearing.

2. **The loop clasp**

Materials:

Round nose plier

Wire of 5 or 6."

Steps

a. Pick the wire of 5 or 6" and use the round nose plier to bend one of the ends of the wire over to about 1.5" from the end

b. Then, make a loop by wrapping the wire ends around the pliers.

c. Then, to finish the wrapping process, hold the bottom of the pliers and complete it.

d. While making the loop, be very sure that the whole is very large to contain the hook you want to use.

e. Turn and bring the wire around and keep rolling the wire in order to make the loop center over the wire.

f. Hold the loop very well with the pliers and wrap the wire up to two to three times.

g. When the loop is fine in shape, clip close it.

h. Peradventure, the wraps are not close together and take the bent nose pliers and pinch everything up.

i. Turn the clipped end to face you, grab and hold the wire above the wrap.

j.   After the grab at length, bend it towards the back

k.   At this point, you will need to make the loop like the time you started. Wrap down the first wrap.

l.   Now you will need to make a clip very close to the first wrap that you've bent.

m.   Then, squeeze smoothly so that the ends of the clip will join together.

This is the end of your clasp. Mind you, there are many things that can be attached to this clasp. In fact, earrings can fit in very well.

LIVER OF SULFUR, POLISHING, AND WAXING OF THE PROJECTS

Liver of Sulfur is, basically, an oxidation agent that is used to add patina to the jewelry created. Basically, LOS is very important because you are dealing with iron and thus, they would surely depreciate with time. LOS, actually, is of two types the gel type and the Lump liver type. The two will as well worn out with time. To create LOS, you will need the following:

For a Lump Liver of Sulfur type:

- Pea-sized lump of LOS
- 1 cup hot (not boiling) distilled water
- 1 cup of cold water
- 1 teaspoon baking soda
- 2 plastic or glass bowls

For the Gel Liver of Sulfur:
- 1 cup hot (not boiling) distilled water
- 1 cup of cold water

- 1 teaspoon baking soda

- 2 plastic or glass bowls

To apply them you will need to dip a paintbrush to get enough of the Gel and add it gradually as if you were painting.

After getting the LOS, the following are the step-by-step guide to how it can be applied to the projects:

Step 1

You are going to prepare more than one bowl. In the first bowl, pick up the prepared LOS, place it directly in relatively hot water.

Step 2

Immediately, keep at stirring the oxidant agent using rubber to avoid being burnt.

Step 3

When you have stirred consistently, you will notice a yellowish color of the water. For now, you are done with the first bowl.

Step 4

You are ready for the second bowl. There, measure a cup full of cold water not hot.

Step 5

Immediately, pick baking soda of about 55mml, add it and stir too. There won't be a change in the color of the water, though. Making you keep stirring until the particles of the soda dissolved –you can monitor it by checking it through the pestle from time to time.

Step 6

The actual reason for the soda is to render the patina in order to debar it from being too dark in color and maintaining its color.

Step 7

The two contents are ready. Gently repeatedly till the color of the jewelry turns to the color you want, dip the jewelry into the hot water first. Make sure you avoid direct contact with the content; it could be toxic, really.

Step 8

Don't panic if the change in color is not instant; the substance works on jewelry gradually and not instant. This is why you'd need to dip the content continually as you monitor the color.

Step 9

Once the color is as dark as you want it, dip it into the cold content; the second bowl. Basically, the cold water will stop the reaction of the LOS and its constituents like the patina on the jewelry. This is the more reason you must be sure the color has got to what you want before dipping it into the second bowl.

Step 10

Then, take it gently and in a simple way and dry it. Take up a paper towel to enhance the drying.

Step 11

There are varying colors depending on the type of wire you have used. For the three projects, they are basically built with base wire of silver and a copper as the warp wire. The copper wire will be a bit darker than the rest. Other colors from the wires including fine silver, sterling, and others will vary.

Step 12

After the dipping and drying, you will need buffing cloth to clean every angle of the jewelry. The effect of the cleaning is so that the patina will be erased totally and make the brightness of the jewelry to be pronounced.

Step 13

Make sure you clean from every space and within the weave so that the patina will leave all the angles of the jewelry.

Step 14

Should it not be bright as you have envisaged, repeat the cleaning process. You can use a clean cloth to hold it as you finish up the cleaning.

Caution

You have to prepare as the thickness of the wire will determine how thorough you will clean the jewelry. The oxidation in copper will be removed quickly than other types of wires, be prepared. Don't at any point have contact with the LOS; it could affect your skin.

POLISHING

Polishing of wire is simply making it brighter. It is an essential part of the jewelry making as they are the latter part that brings out the quality of the work –it can't be neglected. You must be careful with cleaning as it is totally different from polishing. There are different ways you can use to polish your projects as discussed before. Two of these ways include:

Using the hand polishing

The basic thing that you need is a red rouge and a cloth. It is one of the basic technique. You add the rouge on the cloth and clean the jewelry gently. Amazingly, you can do this even before building the work but only make sure you keep the cloth for onward cleaning after the conclusion. After that, you will need the toothpaste now. Add it to the cloth and clean gently. The color of the wires should be shining amazingly now. With warm water, rinse the red rouge off the jewelry. This is one of the cheapest methods because you don't need to buy any special thing. However, you can buy cloth special made for jewelry because it is in-built with red rouge. The work is ready.

Using the Ionic cleaner

This is one of the fastest jewelry polishing technique. Though it could be expensive because of the materials needed, it is one of the safest of all. It works in a special way as the gemstone, such as the one in the earring of the project, does not get broken in the cleaning process. You will apply it gently and make sure it flows in between the wire, especially for the woven wires. After it had got to the corners, pull it out everything. This is all for the technique. Clean it all totally, and the work is ready.

WAXING

This is another special way of preparing the jewelry for usage. Waxing basically prevents the wires from rust. This is done by helping it to maintain its color throughout the usage. This is one of the oldest forms of wire preservation. The steps of applying wax or waxing of the three projects discussed in this book are very necessary. It is pertinent to note that as the processes of preserving wires and enhancing the beauty of jewelry have been discussed, they can be applied in their chronological order. That is, LOS, Polishing, and Waxing can be applied to the same jewelry at different times for the same purpose. To wax, follow these steps:

Step 1

Prepare the jewelry for waxing by using a buff cloth to clean the surface. Make sure every point of the weave is cleansed of dust.

Step 2

Pick the alcohol content and add it to a different cloth

until it is saturated with enough to clean off once the jewelry.

Step 3

Rub the cloth gently on the jewelry round and at every hidden point of the weave.

Step 4

Apply the coating of the wire to polish it round and softly.

Step 5

Leave the jewelry to dry and expose it only to humidity; avoid direct sunlight contact. The beauty is coming showing up already. Let the polish dry off very well.

Step 6

You will need to buff the jewelry now. This can be done using a machine such as a stockinette roll. However, you can use a wool-like cloth to clean gently. If perhaps what you are doing has a quite large surface and are many, use the electric drill to make the work easier and faster.

Step 7

After you have done everything, your work is ready. However, try to repeat the processes again to get the desired results. This is because the waxing might not be obvious really at the first application; the effect is most obvious when the process is repeated.

Every one of the projects is more or less incomplete without proper application of the LOS, polish, and wax respectively. Take note of everything and use your jewelry.

In conclusion, take every one of the additional effects suggested as an advantage to beautify your works. They will give your works the desired professionality, stunning look, and charming usage that will fit very well to your clients desired.

CRAFT WIRE VS. 0.999 FINE SILVER

While making pieces of jewelry using wires, understanding the texture and nature of the wires used is very important. Of this reason is why understanding craft wire and 0.999 fine silver nature is paramount. A craft wire ranges in its softness. A 0.999 fine silver has been a huge source of investment because of its purity and quality. These two wires are commonly used in jewelry making to ensure the sustenance of the work. Though the two wires are very flexible compared to other types of wires, they serve different purposes. This is because craft wires are always very suitable for the base and the fine silver for warp wire.

The size of the wires has been the contributing factor for their difference. Craft wires are between the 16 to 24 gauge and Fine silver ranges from 4 to any length depending on the project at hand. They are very flexible and body friendly. As the base wire, craft wire is very effective because the texture is soft, cool and accommodating for wires to weave on.

The 0.999 fine silver, which also refers to as the three nines, is very good for making curves and bends in jewelry making. The level of its purity is what makes it to be referred to as the .999. It is used because it is coated with silver and thus, durable for long time usage.

The length of craft wire and fine silver are different; they are determined by what the user wants. In their length, one could get different colors tinted around for a suitable bracelet or necklace. For the purity suitable for jewelry making, use the 92.5 percent stamped level of fine silver. The range in level of purity is not applicable to a craft wire.

The two wires are good for jewelry because, in the technique of wire works, there are different bending, cutting, buffing, pulling, etc. which will not be good for just random wires. With these wires, you are sure of durability and amazing friendly usage. The two wires are very easy to manipulate round during works; regardless of the technique, they work effectively.

Whatever the scenario, craft wires are good for base wires, especially in the weaving technique, while fine silver will always be the warp. Warps are always the most noticeable part of jewelry, and because fine silver comes with different colors, you are sure things will be in place without special polishing.

HOW TO SPLICE ON MORE WIRE IF YOU RUN OUT

As a wire weaving jewelry maker, most especially beginner, running out of wire is what happens. This is because a change in wire sizes, inaccurate size estimation, type of wire, and lots more, will affect the end product of the work. Experts might know their way around the scenario, even though it might not be perfect. There are different things to be done but there are few basic things that could give a fast and accurate result. Though splicing, as part of the techniques, has been discussed earlier, understanding how it can be used for manipulation is a special case —why this section is a necessity. As a beginner, you were working and suddenly exhaust your wire, don't panic. The following processes explain how to splice on more wire if you run out. If you are to work towards a finished piece and you are going to do a big long weave. You are going to learn how to end a wire and add a wire if you run out.

Actually, there are two basic things to do while splicing wire: either you run out of wire because you want to start new weave or you run out of wire because you want to end the work.

Note that the steps given here can fit into any of the techniques you are using. In other words, you are the determiner of when to incorporate splicing of the wire. However, no matter the situation, you will always need to end a wire; this is why it is important to know how to splice wire when you run out of it.

TO END A WIRE

Step 1

Once you are at the end of the wire, you need to trim it.

Step 2

Be careful not to trim anyhow because you have a choice of when to trim it. Then take the pointy flush cutter and trim.

Step 3

Observe the wideness of the point you are, do not trim it when it is doing a wide weave. Therefore, hold all the warp wire tight to its base as you trim.

Step 4

Because if you clip the warp wire at the point of wide weave, it could pull out and it would be like a weave that goes up and swing over the wrap wire itself, move away from the wide point. You can reduce the wire backwards to a tight point since you can't continue.

Step 5

Still at the point of trim, you should trim it when it is in a nice tight coil because it has a little knot or acts like a little knot.

Step 6

Move the last coil of the pattern of the weave wire and trim really tight in between the two wrap wires.

Step 7

Trim between the two wrap wires so the tail sat in between. In there, they are nice and safe and will not catch on anything –such as piercing and damaging the skin, damaging clothes, and many more.

Step 8

At this point, you will notice that the trim is on one coil instead of having it at the end of the second coil.

This is because at that point, you can come into the new wire and build the second wire coil at the bottom of the warp wire and then continue so it won't disrupt the flow.

You have to be careful not to leave the tight wires loosed and you might need to start from the beginning. More so, you have to be careful in the process of trimming to not let the warp and the base wires bend.

Step 9

To trim the weave wire, use your pointy flush cutter which will not only allow just the tip on the wire but also let you continue with the coil and weaves.

Step 10

Once you are at a significant distance away from the start of the new wire, you trim the weave start too by trimming it allowing it to sit in between the base wire. Therefore, it is essential you have a very pointy flush cutter.

Caution

Make sure the tail ends are hidden and wouldn't catch on anything. If peradventure you cut it too long, you can trim it again or you could use your chain nose pliers burnish it. The goal is to keep it (the tail) as invisible as possible.

STARTING A NEW WIRE

Adding a new wire is more or less like ending the warp wire (the weaving or adds-on wire). This because the end of the wire is the beginning of the other. Both processes work hand-in-hand; where one ends, the other is expected. The ending of a wire does not necessarily mean you have completed the job, but rather you can suggest the adding of new wire because the other ran out. The following are practical steps to starting a new wire:

Step 1

At the point where you finished your wire, pick a wire of same size and more length. The length is required to avoid the end of the wire. Make sure you straighten the new wire to avoid the rumpling –make it ready for usage.

Note that you must have kept the wires tight together before sorting for the new one.

Step 2

At this point of inserting the wire, check the gap whether it is wide. If it is intact, pull the finished wire to the back and insert the new one from the front.

Step 3

You will need to hold the finished warp wire tightly and with that tightness, insert the new one and continue the weaving.

Step 4

After the weaving has got to a reasonable length, check the point and make sure there is no disparity in the wires, even in the patterns. If otherwise, try to adjust the new wire holding the finished one tight.

Step 5

With the wire intact, trim the two wires together. The wires should be of equal length and not be able to catch on things around it; it could even injure you.

The addition is ready. Incorporate these tricks at every point of your work. Many people say using joining at the point of weaving creates an outstanding effect; this will not be true to you until you try it out. Good luck!

INCORPORATION OF BEADS INTO DESIGNS

At the points and stages of jewelry designs lie the incorporation of beads. Whatever the kind of technique in use, incorporating beads into the design is very easy and done in a simple way.

Step 1

When you get to String a 60 seed bead on each outside of a 20-gauge base wire.

Step 2

The beads must be given in even spacing and add color.

Step 3

Pick the beads and thrust the wires through. Then

repeat the crossing of the next two wires in the center.

Step 4

Bend them to the back, trim, and loop them next to the bead on the outside 20-gauge base wires.

Step 5

Continue to make a pyramid of beads and crossed wires.

Step 6

Trim and tighten each loop when it is in place. The outside 20-gauge wires should cross at the top.

Step 7

Using flat nose pliers, bend in the outside framing wires to echo the angle of the bead pyramid.

Step 8

Cross them at the top, right over left.

Step 9

Wrap the 20-gauge wires around the 14-gauge framing wires twice. Trim the end and pinch tightly.

In another way, you can work with different works than the earrings.

When the jewelry is bracelet, necklace or any other thing, consider using the following steps:

Step 1

Measure and cut a 24-gauge wire to your desired length.

Step 2

At the tip of the round nose pliers, pinch the wire at the center and pull the ends using the plier itself. While making the pull, be sure it results in a small loop. So, the pulling must be in opposite directions.

Step 3

Drop the first loop made, measure and cut three pieces of 20-gauge for base wires.

Step 4

One after the other, pick the base and string the beads you have prepared there until the height of the stringed-beads gets to 1 inch. Repeat this for all the base wires.

Step 5

Then place the first base and the third on the right and left sides respectively.

Step 6

Then, hold the wires with your thumb and slide the small loop created in step 1 to the base wire 2.

Step 7

Put the ends of the wires of the first and third under the warp wire.

Step 8

Then, move the warp wire from the top and take it over the third base wire but very close to the loop and betwixt base wires one and two.

Step 9

With the same wire put in proper bend the beads by moving straight and at the back of the bundle of the wires.

Step 10

Then, move the warp wire from the below over but betwixt base wires two and three. Be careful to ensure that the place to make good bend is opened by making the warp wire very close to the seed beads.

Step 11

At the base wire 2 as well, slide a bead there.

Step 12

As you've done before, take the warp wire betwixt

and over the base wires one and two. Maintain the kind of pattern you have created from the beginning.

Step 13

Pick the wire and pull it towards the back to make a bend.

Step 14

Then, pick the warp from below, and take it over the bundle and put it betwixt base wires two and three.

Step 15

Don't drop the wire yet, take it to the back to make a bend.

The work is ready. Make sure you move towards the kind of jewelry you are making. Repeating the steps might be the best option.

HELPFUL TIPS FOR WIRE WEAVING

1. Learn to improvise: You do not, necessarily, need to buy expensive tools for every jewelry project and work. Basic household objects can be used, sometimes. Use household objects for shaping jewelry. For example, you can use a round barreled pencil or pen to straighten your wire. You can do this by placing the wire between your thumb and the pen then pull the wire through several times. Bottles can make bracelets' mandrels, just be careful not to hammer them.

2. Keep your weaves kink-free: If due to a mistake you need to unwrap a section of the weave, be sure to straighten and smoothen out that section before you continue weaving. To avoid breakage, make sure your weave is kink-free. And if there is a link, straighten it out right away. A kink is a potential weak point that can lead to a break.

3. Your hands, your best tool: As much as possible, resist from always grabbing a tool to do all of your work. Your hands can do it better. Appreciate your best tool but remember to take breaks and stretch your hands as often as possible too.

4. Create a buffer between your fingers and the wire: Create a buffer using a pliable fabric tape so as to reduce the friction between your fingers directly against the wire. Letting the wire move constantly over your fingers can cause an injury or wear due to heat from friction.

5. Keep your base wire evenly spaced: it is not easy to do, but it is important to keep an equal distance between the base wires. When weaving, you can space the point at which you're weaving till about half an inch then allow it spread and flare out to allow you weave easily. If holding onto the wire with your hands is not working so well yet, make use of a wooden ring clamp. It secures all the wires in place without marking them. With just the strength of your fingers, the wires are held in place.

6. Make them tight and fitted: Pull the weaving wire tightly against each frame wire with every wrap. Make sure the weaving wire lies perfectly flat when it travels across two frame wires. Push the weaves together too! Tension is necessary when weaving. If your weaves are too tight, you will pull your base wires out of shape. But leaving it loose, you have uneven spacing between your wrap wires.

7. Round-nose pliers can be used as mandrels: Round-nose pliers can be used to create loops before shaping the wire further. To form a loop, position the round-nose pliers where you would like to make a large loop, leaving the round-nose pliers open. Grip the end of the wire with your fingers and wrap the wire around the jaw of the round-nose pliers.

Remove the pliers and continue to shape the rest of the wire with your finger.

8. A sampler is of great importance: Deciding on which weave to use for a project can be tasking and confusing. So to help you get started on a wire weaving project, make a sampler. Make all different weave styles and make sure each has a loop (on the folded side). With the loop, attach the weaves to a safety pin. This is to give you easy access and this way you would not lose any.

9. Make sure the maintenance of all your equipment is always done at stipulated and continuous times. This means that every iron part of the equipment like pliers will need oil at every point to prevent it from rusting.

SKILL BUILDING EXERCISES

While doing some of the techniques most especially the weaving and wrapping, you must have noticed the pains you sustained. Also, while using the cutter and the pliers –in fact the equipment –you will or might sustain some injuries too. Additionally, doing the skills might be awkward at times because you are not used to them –this is normal. These and other reasons necessitated this section. Therefore, in this section, there will be suggested skill-building exercises that would help you make your hand flexible, reduce pains after long work, and many other things that might be an object of challenge through wire weaving works. These building exercises include:

Stringing large-hole items

This involves stringing something on a large-hole with an ending. You could enhance and make free your hands by just picking up a tough wire and create a large-hole (loop). With the loop, begin the stringing of the wires together till you achieve a considerable length even though you couldn't finish the dead ends. Don't forget that refining the motor skills is what you attain with consistent practice of this exercise.

Stringing smaller beads

Likewise, you could be able to string small beads even with the large holes like the first exercise given. To start, use a yarn with finished ends, perhaps with a tape or a plastic lacing and wrap to a large loop. With this exercise, you can get more effective with the way you swing your hand while weaving. In fact, you can get complex painting pasta and or creating paper beads.

Making a friendship bracelet

With this exercise, you could get on the original jewelry; bracelet. Working with the bracelet for improvement, you will make it personal in the sense that bigger bracelet can be reduced –and smaller ones too –to your size. Here as well, you will need to practice painting the bracelet to the color that you want never buy paints without a proper guide. Like the processing of adding LOS, you can polish the bracelet just to get you much more ready even for subsequent works. While you are not really creating a novel work, your painting, coloring, polishing, etc. skills are enhanced.

Adding buttons to a bracelet

You can pick a common bracelet which could enable stringing buttons to it and get on it. Make sure you are using the basic technique while adding thee buttons. In fact, this exercise is sportive as every button added could create a great sensation, even for a novel pattern. This is an exercise that would increase your skill of using button and clasp while making jewelry. You could make it a style that at every bracelet you made, there will be enough button to stunt the style.

Making incessant loops and earrings connection

This exercise is recommended because while making earring connection with loops, it is very difficult to maintain the wires held together. The skill that will enhance is gripping alongside holding within a given range, the wires while making loops and even earrings connection. This will make you more creative, smart and intelligent in handling wires to connect earrings. The project on earrings is the best example for you to notice the point where you could practice this skill. You could proceed with seashell earrings and flower necklace because many of them are crafted with lots of sewing skills that will enable your creativity, especially your connection of earrings.

Using only 1 wire

With just a single wire, you could fold it and make weaving for a considerable long time. While this might not fetch you all the skills, you will understand the texture of your wire and the best way to handle them. If you understand your wire, you will know how to and when to buy your wires for work. Apart from this, there will be lots of technique to practice while starting or ending a wire. This is very effective during leisure time. There is no time to be checking for wires in a special way, most times when you have a good number of works to do. This is very much effective for everyone. In fact, you could wrap the wire in whatever way you like it. Loose the wire and repeat the same thing you are doing until you achieve.

Swinging wires with different sizes

This exercise is done by simply swinging wires around one another for a good number of times. Make sure you have wires of different sizes and shape so that weaving speed will increase, even with accuracy. This does not really suggest just rolling wires without making the wires straighten, rather, dwindling the wires at different but specific directions. This will enhance your weaving skill. Likewise, the hand flexibility will be there at any point you are while doing the wire works. This is not specific to some techniques, but general to every point.

 Rounding off this section, the exercises that would improve your skills could be personal. Therefore, you might need to understand the problem you are facing. To say, differences in human and their perception coupled with strength will be of greater consideration while selecting exercises; especially effective ones at that. For instance, a southpaw will surely follow different directions at weaving, overlapping, and moving round the wires –compared to a right-handed person. The bottom line is that while taking these exercises will do lots, understanding perfectly who you are and your strength will do much more.

In conclusion, these skills are suggested to improve your moving and handling of the wires to achieve the best and desired results.

CONCLUSION

In conclusion, wire work is one of the most domesticated but lucrative skills that can be done by anyone at any point in time. This is because it requires only some basic techniques and readily available materials. In this book, we have exhaustively explained all you need to know about wire weaving.

The techniques discussed are very simple to apply. There is no need for prior knowledge as this book is for beginners; though it takes into consideration every level of knowledge in wire works. The step by step guide on the techniques in the book makes everything easier and beautiful.

Anyone who wants a job on wire works, even outside the ones discussed here, will need the knowledge of this book. Amazingly, it is like a glance of only cogent information of jewelry making. It is advisable to, for effectiveness sake, work as you read. With this, the total utility and intention of this book will be fulfilled.

Over time, there had barely been, according to statistics of jewelry making through wire works, a book that is summary in nature but very useful for everyone. This book is solely for business if you know what that means.

Before reading the bulky part of this book, read the materials section in order to get them ready. Don't panic; you will be taken through the journey of wire works. Stay glued to knowledge!

HELPFUL LINKS TO LEARN MORE

https://www.beaducation.com

 https://www.youtube.com/wireworks

https://www.jewelrymaking.about.com/od/wiretechniquesinfo/ss/052608.htm

https://www.youtube.com/watch?v=lfy3mLLAMIE

https://www.studiodax.wordpress.com/2011/01/16/i-heart-hearts/

https://www.jewellrymakingjournal.com/wire-wrap-rings-tutorial/

https://www.goodconverters.com

https://www.firemoutaingems.com

https://www.youtube.com/watch?v=s9mSfXyeTOY

Intermediate Wire Weaving

How to Create Wire Jewelry Without Splurging on Expensive Metals

Introduction

There's nothing that satisfies the creativity bug quite like making handcrafted, tangible, beautiful items. Artistic outlets come in all shapes and sizes, but some offer more rewarding end results than others. Wire weaving is one such outlet.

Wire weaving is a jewelry-making technique that is used to create both charmingly simple and stunningly complex designs, and if you're reading this, then you've clearly fallen in love with the craft. As one of the oldest techniques for making jewelry still practiced to this day, there's a lot of information out there regarding which weaves to use, what projects to make, and the many variations of materials you can utilize in order to come up with your own unique pieces. It almost becomes overwhelming to sort it all out, especially once you're past the beginner stages. That's where *Intermediate Wire Weaving* comes in.

This guide offers step by step instructions that teach you more advanced weaves, including over-under, circular, and bezel wire, among others. You'll also be able to put your newfound knowledge of these weaves into practice with the projects laid out in Chapter 2. From brooch pins to ear cuffs, you'll discover a world of possibilities that will open up once you have a few weave patterns under your belt. This book will cover everything needed to successfully complete these projects, from the type of wire you need to the weaves you'll be using. If you're not familiar with what is considered to be the "beginner" weaves, I encourage you to pick up a book on beginner techniques or do some research and master the basics first. You'll understand the intermediate weaves and more difficult projects better if you have a firm grasp of the essential weaves that act as the foundation.

After you master the intermediate weaves found in this book and tackle a few projects, you'll more than likely want to take your creations to the next level by making them uniquely yours. Personalization will be discussed later on, along with common problems that you might encounter while wire weaving and how to solve them. Don't get discouraged if you find one of the projects or weaves to be more difficult than others. Mastery takes practice! There wouldn't be any fun in it if you were an expert from the get-go, would there be?

Additionally, in this book, you will learn about cold connections - how to join two pieces of metal without using heat as with soldering and welding - and discover how to make your own findings.

There's a wealth of knowledge to be had in the following pages, and you'll be guided every step of the way. So roll up your sleeves, pull out your supplies, and keep reading to find out more about the art of intermediate wire weaving.

Chapter 1: Weaves

Let's jump right in and talk about the weaves you'll need to progress to the intermediate projects found in this book and those that can be discovered online. Each style discussed is classic and one that is used for many creations. They will serve you well as you continue to grow your skills and learn more about wire weaving. Since you'll be practicing to start out, you can use any wire material you'd like. Copper is generally best because it's easy to handle and relatively inexpensive. You don't have to worry too much about measurements just yet, either, since we're learning how to do these weaves and not making something that requires set lengths.

Circular Weave

Also known as "coiling", this technique is particularly useful when you're working with rounded pendants and other circular items that are typically difficult to design around. While wire wrapping is generally the most popular method for forming frames around center stones, circular weaving creates intricate and visually stunning patterns that enhance the look of the entire piece.

Tools and materials needed:

- Coiling Gizmo

- 1 spool of 28 gauge round dead soft wire for base coil (you won't use the whole spool, but it's best to have more than enough when using the Coiling Gizmo)

- 24 gauge round dead soft for inner wire, cut to 30 inches

- 1 spool of 20 gauge wire (again, you won't use all of it, but it's better to have excess than to cut it too short)

- Wire cutters

Steps:

There are two ways you can do coiling, but we're

going to cover the simplest method, which requires a Coiling Gizmo. These are extremely useful and relatively inexpensive. They help you create uniform coils without having to do it all by hand, which means the finished product will look more polished and professional. If you prefer to coil by hand, then that's fine, too, of course; you can skip step one and go straight to step three if you'd rather not use a gizmo.

1. Using your Coiling Gizmo, coil the 28 gauge wire until you have a piece that's about 15 inches in length. This is the main coil that you'll be weaving around a base wire.

2. If you skipped step one, your coil should already have an inner wire, and you can proceed to step three. If you used the gizmo, you'll need to thread your 24 gauge wire through the coil. You'll want this wire to be about double the length of the coiled wire, so 30 inches should be enough.

3. Pull the 24 gauge wire through until you have about 1 ½ - 2 inches sticking out from one side of the coil. Next, take your 20 gauge wire and unwind a good long piece - about 12 inches should suffice to start with. Don't cut the wire because you'll need a lot more, but you'll want to have enough to work with without it getting tangled up in excess wire.

4. Start a few inches down the 20 gauge wire so you have something to grip while you're weaving, and begin wrapping the 1 ½ - 2-inch tail from your 24 gauge wire around the 20 gauge wire. You only need to wrap a few times to secure it. Once you feel like it's secure enough, you can slide the coil up so it's flush against the 20 gauge wire.

5. Now comes the fun part. Take your 28 gauge coil and coil it around the 20 gauge wire, making sure each wrap is flush against the one before it. Keep coiling

until you run out of the 28 gauge length, then take the remaining 24 gauge inner wire and wrap it around the 20 gauge a few times to secure it on that end. You can snip off the excess wire so that the lengths are equal on both ends (you should have a few inches of 20 gauge on each side). Pinch down the 24 gauge on either side so that it looks clean and polished with no wires sticking out at odd angles.

You can either stop here and use your finished coil on a project, or you can do one more coil using the 20 gauge wire and wrap it in between the 28 gauge coils so that it's sitting in the grooves. This is purely decorative and entirely optional.

Over-Over Weave

The next two weave styles are versatile in that you can use as many base wires as you want. For the over-over weave, we'll stick with three wires for the purposes of this guide, but just know that you can adjust according to your needs and project requirements.

Tools and materials needed:

- Three 20 gauge base wires (or larger if you prefer), round and dead soft

- 28 gauge weaving wire (again, can be larger or smaller based on your preference), round and dead soft

- Wire cutters

Steps:

1. Cut your three base wires as long as you wish as your only purpose is to get the hang of the weave.

2. Cut a good long length of weaving wire - between 12 and 24 inches should be enough to start with.

3. Secure your weaving wire to the bottom

base wire by wrapping around once, leaving a bit of a tail to hold onto as you continue weaving.

4. With the weaving wire underneath the bottom base wire and pointing toward you, wrap it over the bottom two wires twice, making sure to slide each wrap down toward your fingers to remove any gaps.

5. Now, with the weaving wire under the middle base wire facing toward you, wrap it up over the middle and top wires twice.

6. The weaving wire will now be under all three wires facing toward you. Wrap it up over the bottom two wires again, over the top two, and continue until you're happy with the length or until you have run out of wire.

Keep in mind that you needn't only wrap the weaving wire twice; you can do it three times, five times, ten times, or as many times as you'd prefer. A simple variation such as this will give your pattern a unique look.

Over-Under Weave

Once again, you can use any number of base wires, but we'll teach you how to do this weave with six. This pattern seems complicated at first, but it's fairly straightforward and only requires that you keep track of whether you're going over or under.

Tools and materials needed:

- Six 20 gauge base wires (or larger/smaller), round and dead soft

- 28 gauge weaving wire (or larger/smaller), round and dead soft

- wire cutters

Steps:

1. Fan out your six base wires so that you

have space to weave the wire in and out. There's a lot of movement to this weave, so you'll want to give yourself enough space to prevent getting tangled up.

2. Cut 12 to 24 inches of your weaving wire. Secure it by leaving a short tail for you to hold onto, and wrap it over the bottom wire.

3. Wrap your wire once around the bottom two wires going from bottom to top, ending with the wire over the top of and behind the second wire from the bottom (it might help to assign your wires numbers - bottom 1, then 2, and so on up to your top wire, 6).

4. Wrap once around base wires 2 and 3, again going from bottom to top and ending behind the third wire. Then wrap around wires 3 and 4, then 4 and 5, and finally wires 5 and 6. End with your weaving wire behind all the wires facing

toward you.

5. Bring your weaving wire to the front between wires 4 and 5 and wrap once around wire 5. Then bring the weaving wire to the front between wires 3 and 4 and wrap once around wire 4. Continue following this pattern for wires 3 and 2.

6. Once you've wrapped around wire 2, bring the weaving wire down behind wire 1 and wrap up and over the bottom two wires, just like in step three.

7. Repeat step three, wrapping wires 1 and 2, 2 and 3, 3 and 4, 4 and 5, and 5 and 6.

8. Repeat step five, wrapping one wire at a time as you make your way back down.

Keep going until you're happy with the length or until you run out of wire.

Bezel Wire Weave

There are a few different weaves you can use when you're making a frame, or bezel, for a pendant necklace. Some are very basic and simple, while others are more complex and involved. The one we're going to look at is a little more intricate and on the fancier side. It forms a very sturdy frame for large stones and offers a more interesting appearance than frames created using simple wire wrapping techniques. You'll have to adjust sizing based on your specific project, but for now, we'll just go through the basic how to. In the next chapter, we'll look at some uses for these weaves and get into the nitty-gritty of tools, materials, and sizing.

Tools and materials needed:

- Three 8-inch 20 gauge base wires of round and dead soft (longer or shorter is fine; you just want enough that you can get the hang of the pattern)

- 24 inches of 28 gauge weaving wire, round and dead soft

- Wire cutters

Steps:

1. Find roughly the center of your wires, and hold onto the bunch there, fanning out the wires on the side you'll be weaving.

2. Place your weaving wire between the bottom wire and the one just above it, holding onto a small section to secure it. Wrap it once around the bottom wire going from top to bottom. Your weaving wire should now be behind the base wires facing up toward the top ones.

3. Wrap your weaving wire between the top two wires, pull it down, and then repeat (from behind, bring the weaving wire to the front between the top two wires). This creates two wraps around the

bottom two wires.

4. Next, wrap the top two wires by bringing your weaving wire up and over the top, and then between the bottom two wires.

5. Wrap the top wire once by going up over the top, and then bring the weaving wire to the back by going between the top two wires.

6. Wrap around the top two wires again twice, and then wrap around the bottom two wires twice so that your weaving wire ends up in the front.

7. Make one wrap on the bottom wire as you did for the top, ending with the wire in the back and pointing down. Your pattern should look something like this so far, with the colon representing single loops:

||:||

|| ||: (2, 2, loop, 2, 2, loop)

8. Keep following the pattern: wrap bottom two twice, top two twice, single loop, top two twice, bottom two twice, and then loop.

There will be more steps when you're using this frame to actually make something, but for now, that's the gist of it.

Diagonal Wire Weave

When you need a simplistic but lovely design that's adaptable and can be made with as many or as few base wires as you want, a diagonal weave should be your go-to. We're going to show you how to create this pattern with two wires, but you can work up to four if you'd like.

Tools and materials needed:

- Two 8-inch 20 gauge base wires, round and dead soft or half hard

- 24 inches of 28 gauge weaving wire, round and dead soft

Steps:

1. **As** usual, take your two base wires and wrap your weaving wire over the bottom one to secure it. It should go front to back and end up behind the bottom wire pointing down.

2. **Wrap** your weaving wire over both base wires, going from the bottom to the top, then bring it between the wires and up around just the top wire.

3. **Bring** the weaving wire behind both wires, then pull it up and over the bottom wire, just like you did in step one. Then, wrap up and over both wires as in step two, and finish by wrapping over the top wire once.

4. **Repeat** the pattern: single wrap bottom, wrap both, single wrap top, and back to bottom.

This is by no means an exhaustive list of

intermediate weaves. There are many techniques out there, so it would be impossible to list them all. Many of these weaves also have different names associated with them, making it even more difficult to parse them out. But you don't need to worry about any of that. Just master these weaves, and learning each one along with the beginner knowledge you already possess will be enough to help you craft incredibly detailed and stunningly simple designs. To get started using these patterns firsthand, continue on to the next (and highly anticipated) chapter - projects!

Chapter 2: Projects

It's time to get to the good stuff. Putting your skills to good use is the most rewarding part of learning a new hobby. Wire weaving is great that way, because you get to wear or gift your finished product; Christmas and birthdays just got a whole lot easier.

All of the following projects utilize beginner weaves that you should already be familiar with as well as intermediate weaves that are covered in Chapter 1. In addition, they don't require any special tools or materials that are ridiculously expensive.

So, without further ado, let's get crafting.

Woven Bezel Pendant

Remember the bezel wire weave you just learned about in the previous chapter? Well, you already get to put it to good use.

Tools and materials needed:

- Wire cutters

- Flat or round nose pliers

- Bail making pliers

- 20 gauge copper wire, round and dead soft

- One spool 28 gauge copper weaving wire, round and dead soft

- Cabochon of the size and shape of your choosing

Steps:

1. To first figure out what length your 20 gauge base wires should be and how many you will need, take your cabochon and wrap enough wire around it so that it covers the perimeter - then triple that length. You want it to be long enough that you can use the excess length to secure the pendant and make a bail. You

should also estimate how many wires you need based on the width of the sides of the cabochon. You'll generally need three or four. Once you have your measurements, cut your base wires.

2. Using the **bezel wire weave** described in Chapter 1, start in the middle of the base wires, and work your way up one side. Periodically check to make sure the frame isn't too long or larger than your stone; it needs to fit snugly or it will pop out.

3. At three points of your weave, you'll make a large loop that will be used later to secure your cabochon. These points will be at the center of the side, bottom, and the other side center of the cabochon. Once you've woven to the first point, the center of the first side, ensure you're at a point where your weaving wire is at/over the top wire. After you've woven around the top two wires and are

about to make your single loop around just the top wire, use two fingers and wrap the wire around them **while** you make your single loop. All you're trying to do is leave a little slack in the wire which you'll use later.

4. Keep following the bezel weave pattern until you reach your second point at the spot where the bottom center of the stone will be. Create another loop the same way you did in the previous step. Continue on and do the same loop on the other side center opposite the first loop. Make sure each loop is on the same base wire - (the top one).

5. Once you've woven to the correct length (the perimeter of your cabochon), set your stone down on a flat surface so that you can more easily shape your frame around it. You need to place the frame around the stone so that the loops are facing outward. Press down and pat the

frame down gently so it forms around the stone. At either end of the weave where your unwoven base wires show, squeeze those wires inward so that the ends closest to the weave shape around the top of your stone. Ensure the stone can't pop through the front of the frame. We'll take care of the back soon.

6. Now it's time to close your frame. Take the front two wires on either side of the front of your frame and cross them over each other where they go into the weave. You're essentially forming an X at the very top of your frame. Bend those wires toward the back, then cross them into an X again at the back top of the frame.

7. You should still have your weaving wire coming off one side of the frame. Don't cut that off the spool yet - you're going to need it. You should also now have four base wires (two on either end of the frame) since we bent two ends out of the

way. Using the same pattern we made the frame with, weave them together until you have a length that's long enough to bend around into a bail. End your weaving wire by wrapping it a few times around a single base wire, then cut it close to the base wire. Use pliers to pinch the tail down to the base wire so it's not sticking out.

8. Using bail making pliers (or your hand if you don't have any), bend the top weave over to form the standard bail shape.

9. It's now time to set the stone, so place your frame on a flat surface face down and set your cabochon in it. Take the wires you formed an X with and lay them so that they're forming an X over your stone. They don't have to be centered, but each wire should be near the loop that's on its respective side.

10. Take one of the loops that you made

while weaving, flatten it out so it's no longer open, and wrap it around one of the X wires. Once you've wrapped the loop around a few times, you can cut it off and use your pliers to flatten it against the X wire. Do the same thing on the other side with the second loop. Don't cut either of the wires forming the X.

11. Cross the wires again at the bottom of the pendant and, using pliers, thread the bottom loop over and under them, wrapping the same way you did with the side wires. This will be a little more difficult since the wires are closed, but with pliers, it shouldn't be too taxing. Once you've wrapped the bottom loop around the X wires a few times, cut it and flatten it like the others. You can now cut the X wires as well. Try to loop them and tuck them in on themselves so there aren't any ends poking out.

12. Secure the wires coming from the bail by

wrapping them creatively around the X wires in any way you want. You don't want to just cut them, because they're holding your bail together. At least one set should attach somewhere on the back, but the other two can be cut short and tucked under or looped over on themselves to hide the ends.

You are all finished. You now have a gorgeous pendant to show off, put on a chain, or give to someone special.

Wire Woven Brooch Pin

Brooch pins are surprisingly simple to make and can be personalized in several different ways. You can even get creative with this design and add your own embellishments.

Tools and materials needed:

- Wire cutters

- Round nose pliers

- Needle file

- 8.5 inches of 18 gauge copper round half hard wire

- 45 inches of 20 gauge copper round dead soft wire

- 12.5 feet of 26 gauge copper round dead soft wire (you may need to use more or less, depending on embellishments)

- Center stone vertically drilled, about 32mm

- Liver of sulfur and paintbrush (optional)

Steps:

1. The first thing we're going to do is make and shape the brooch pin. In this example, we'll shape it into a flower by making four petals, but you can use any shape you want. Take your 8.5-inch piece of 18 gauge wire and use your nose pliers to shape four rounded petals (or

whatever design you want) on one end of the wire, leaving a nice long stem that will be the pin.

2. Take your needle file, and use it to sharpen the end of the pin. Rotate the pin as you file so the point is even. At this point, you can either add embellishments to the flower pin or move on to the bead frame.

3. For your base wires, you'll need three 12-inch pieces of 20 gauge wire. For your weaving wire, cut 45 inches of the 26 gauge wire.

4. Using either the **over-over** weave or the **diagonal** weave, start 4 inches from one end of the base wires and begin weaving. Follow your chosen pattern until you have about 4 inches of weave. If you have a center stone that's larger or smaller than the 32mm recommended, you may have to weave more or less. Once you

have enough to wrap around the perimeter, shape your frame around the stone, and ensure each woven end meets at the top of the bead above the pre-drilled hole.

5. Cut 9 inches of your 20 gauge wire and use it to string the center stone, then place your stone in your frame. You'll need to thread the 20 gauge wire through the bottom of your frame so that you can secure the center stone in a later step. Leave about 1 inch of the 20 gauge wire sticking out the bottom.

6. To close the top of your frame around the bead, pinch the base wires together around the wire that's going through your stone, and use your excess wrapping wire to wrap the whole bundle. Once you're done wrapping, tuck any excess tails into the frame or wrap.

7. The next step is optional and requires a

small, 5mm bead. Separate the base wires from the center wire, and use the center wire to make a few more wraps around the one you did in step 6. When you have 2 inches of wire left to wrap, string a 5mm bead so that it's facing what will be the front. Finish wrapping, then tuck in any excess wire.

8. Now we're going to use the base wires to make "wings" around the center stone. Separate them so you have three shaped into a wing on one side and three on the other. They should be spread out side to side rather than bunched up. Thread them through their respective sides of the frame, then down through the bottom of it. If you want to add beads or other embellishments to the wires sticking out from the bottom, feel free; otherwise, you can trim them and loop them around so they wrap against the frame.

9. Now we're going to weave the wings, and, again, you have your choice of pattern. You can use any technique discussed in Chapter 1, or you can choose to go with something else you're familiar with. Start from the top and weave until you get to the back where all the frame wires meet. Trim and tuck excess wire.

10. Repeat step 9 on the other wing.

11. If you want to add any embellishments from here, go for it; otherwise, take the pin you made in the first steps and slip it through the wings behind the center stone, and you just made a brooch pin.

Braided Wire Woven Cuff Bracelet

Cuff bracelets are super easy to make, but the end result is amazing. This uses a braiding technique that's fairly beginner-level, but the use of nine base wires makes it a little more complex. Like the brooch pin, it's easily customizable; you can add beads, extra wire designs, or fancy swirls and loops - anything you want, really.

Tools and materials needed:

- 9 pieces of 10.5-inch 20 gauge round dead soft wire, either sterling silver or copper (though silver looks best with this design)

- Masking tape

- Round nose pliers

- Wire cutters

Steps:

1. Line up all nine strands of your wire and use your masking tape to hold them together on one end. Separate your wires into groups of 5 and 4 by slightly bending one group to the side and the other group to the other side.

2. Hold your wires so that the masking tape

end is facing toward you and the side with five wires is on the right. Starting with the outermost wire on the right side, weave it over two wires, then under two wires to bring it over to the other side. You should now have four wires where you had five, and five wires where you had four.

3. Once again, from the left side this time, take the outermost wire and weave it over two then under two. The two wires that have been braided should now form an X towards the bottom, and you should again have five wires on the side that originally had five and four on the other.

4. Keep following this pattern of weaving over two and under two. As you progress, you'll see the bracelet starting to form a nice design of roughly diamond-shaped spaces and rounded edges. Continue weaving until you have around two inches of wire left.

5. Now it's time to finish off the ends. Don't worry if all your wire ends are different lengths. Trim the outermost wires on either side to about 1 inch, then coil them inward using your round nose pliers until they form a spiral. Curl it over the top edge of your design so that it holds the outer strands in place. Your outer wires should be coming from underneath the others, so if you curl them over they'll secure the sides of the bracelet. Try to make both spirals level with one another.

6. Curl the rest of your wires inward using spirals to secure the ends. You don't have to do them in any particular order, as long as they all are on the same side of the bracelet.

7. Once you've finished one side, remove the masking tape from the other side and splay out your wires. If your bracelet is too short to wrap comfortably around your wrist, continue your braid on the

end that had the tape. If it's long enough, cut the wires to the same lengths you had on the other side and spiral them inward just as you did in steps 5 and 6.

Now, you're done. That wasn't so hard, was it? Once you get the hang of this design, you can add beads at various intervals along the braid or even on the ends of the spirals. Get creative, and see what you can come up with.

Wire Woven Filigree Earrings

The word "filigree" might make this sound more intimidating, but it's just a fancier style that gives your earrings a delicate, almost fantasy quality. You can make the whole thing wire and not add any beads to it, but for this project, we're going to tell you how to add a small accent crystal.

Tools and materials needed:

- 4 pieces of 7-inch 20 gauge copper round

dead soft wire

- 1 spool of 26 or 28 gauge copper round dead soft wire

- Round nose pliers

- 2 small crystals or beads (5mm or smaller)

- Ear wires or extra wire to make your own

Steps:

1. Start about two inches from one end of two your 20 gauge base wires. The weave we're going to use is a modified **bezel** weave. Instead of having single wraps on both the top and bottom wire, we're just going to single wrap the bottom. So, to start, wrap both wires twice, then the bottom wire **four times**. Then wrap both wires twice and the bottom wire four times. Your pattern should look something like this (dots represent single wraps):

||....||....||....||

2. Continue with the pattern until you have **eighteen** double wraps (||), then add **eight** single wraps to the bottom wire (........). The end weave should look like this: (||........).

3. Bend your top base wire into a tight loop so that it folds back on itself rather than forward, then realign it with the bottom base wire. The loop should be above the eight single wraps.

4. Continue on with your pattern, starting with two double wraps and four single wraps. Keep going until you have **five** double wraps, but this time don't add the four single wraps after the last double. Instead, wrap around the top wire a few times to secure your weave.

5. Using the loop you created with the base wire as your topmost point, bend the frame you've made into a U shape. Now

take the side that has the most weaves (the end you started with) and, starting at the 6th double wrap, bend that end upward to form an upside down U. The 6th double wrap should be the bottom-most point.

6. On the end you started weaving, you should have a short tail left by your weaving wire. Wrap that around a few times to secure it, and then trim it and flatten it against the base wire.

7. You should now have two base wires pointing down and two pointing up. Bend your base wires inward so that they all point toward the finished side of the frame. Trim your wires so that the innermost ones touch the inside of the frame and the outermost wires reach slightly past the frame. Curl the outermost wires so that the ends form little spirals that fit within the frame. Do the same with the innermost wires, but

curl them a little tighter so that they're closer to the opposite side of the frame from the other spirals.

8. Your weaving wire should still be connected. If it isn't, you'll have to wrap a new one on. Either way, keep doing single loops (on one of the innermost wires forming a tight spiral) until you're about midway up the spiral.

9. At this point, you'll need to cut your weaving wire off the spool to make the next wrap easier. Thread the end of your weaving wire through the tight spiral so that it comes out of the back, then begin weaving around the outermost spiral that's behind the spiral you started with. Keep wrapping until your weaving wire has reached the point where the spiral touches the inner edge of the frame, then make two double wraps around both the frame and the outermost spiral to attach it. Next, return to making the single

loops going around the spiral until you've reached about midway (this should only take four or five wraps). Trim and flatten/pinch down the wire.

10. To do the same on the other two spirals, cut a long length of weaving wire and follow the same wrapping pattern you did in steps 8 and 9 with one modification - when you've woven the tighter spiral to the point where it almost touches the other tight spiral, weave once around the other spiral to connect the two, then continue your single wraps.

11. Before you reach the end of the longer outermost spiral, if you want to attach a crystal, get to about midway up the outermost wire then thread your bead onto your weaving wire. Once the crystal is in between the two sets of spirals (in the middle of your earring), wrap a couple of times around the outermost spiral you already wrapped in step 9 to

secure the crystal and wire in place. Then, thread it through the bead again to bring your wire back to the unfinished spiral. Keep wrapping the outermost spiral in the same way as in step 9.

12. Repeat steps 1-11 to create the second earring. Attach ear wires to both, and then you are finished.

Wire Tree Pendant

Unquestionably, one of the most iconic symbols for jewelry is the tree of life. So, it only makes sense that you should learn how to work it into your wire weaving designs.

Tools and materials needed:

- 16 gauge copper round dead soft wire (length varies based on the stone being used)
- 1 spool of 26 gauge copper round dead soft wire

- 14 pieces of 24 gauge copper round dead soft wire, with each piece double the length of your center stone

- Large center stone; 2 inches is a good size to start with

- Wire cutters

- Round nose pliers

- Bezel making pliers

- Masking tape

Steps:

1. Cut a length of 16 gauge wire that's three times the length of your center stone. Start shaping the wire around your stone by placing the bottom of your stone at the center of the wire and forming the wire around it. You should have roughly equal ends overlapping at the top of the stone, and you want the frame to be just a touch larger than your stone. Once you have

the right size, bend your wires outward slightly at the top where they meet at the top of the stone. This marks your end points and where you will make the bail.

2. We're going to weave the bail first so that the frame stays in the correct shape. Make sure your base wires are separated by about a quarter of an inch or however wide you want your bail to be. Use the pattern of your choice for the bail - you can do a modified **bezel** weave, **diagonal** weave, modified **over-over**, or anything else you would like. Just as in the first project (pendant), weave until you have a long enough length that you can bend it over into a bail using your bail making pliers. Don't cut your excess wire coming from the bail just yet; you'll need them to secure the stone. Bend them into any shape that suits you, as long as it's in such a way that it will prevent the stone from popping out. You

can finish off the ends into spirals if you so desire. Just make sure they're touching the frame so you can secure them to it.

3. Now, it's time for the tree. Take your 14 pieces of 24 gauge wire and hold them in a bundle so the ends are aligned. Using your round nose pliers, start twisting about a third of the way down to form the roots and bottom of the trunk. Then take smaller sections of the wire on the other side (opposite the roots) and twist them to make branches. This is where you have the opportunity to get creative, because you can make your tree look any way you want. Occasionally, you should hold your tree up to the stone to see if you like the look. Don't twist all the way to the ends of the wire as you'll need some length to secure the tree to the frame.

4. The first part you want to attach is the roots. Take a nice big piece of masking

tape and lay it on the back of your frame, and then set your stone in. You should have a couple long ends of tape on either side of the frame. Use these to secure your tree down, but don't get any tape on the roots since you want to work with those.

5. Using your pliers, thread each individual root through the frame and wrap them around several times to secure them. If you made loops with the excess base wire in the back, don't forget to wrap some of the roots around those to secure them to the frame as well. When you're done, trim and tuck any root wires that are sticking out.

6. Now we're going to secure the branches. Fan them out into whatever arrangement you want, then attach the excess wire coming from the branches just as you did with the roots. Again, if your base wires are touching the frame in any place

where you're securing branches, also wrap the wires around these to attach them to the frame as well. Trim and tuck the tails of any branch wires and make sure you're happy with the way the branches are arranged.

You are now done. That's all it takes to make a gorgeous and unique tree of life pendant.

Wire Woven Ring

This last project is incredibly customizable. You can use any weaving technique you want, and you will make a frame for a center stone to add on, finishing it up with some pretty spirals or really anything else.

Tools and materials needed:

- 2-3 pieces of 20 gauge copper round dead soft wire, cut to roughly 3.5 inches

- 3 feet of 28 gauge copper round dead soft wire

- Wire cutters

- Ring sizer (or just your own finger)

- Round nose pliers

Steps:

1. Starting with your 20 gauge base wires, begin wrapping the 28 gauge weaving wire in any pattern you want. The number of base wires you use depends on both the pattern you want and the width you'd like the ring to be. Feel free to exercise your creative freedom here.

2. Weave your chosen pattern until the length is long enough to wrap around into your desired ring size. You'll want to periodically check to see how you're doing, because if you weave too much, your ring will be too big. Once you've woven the proper length, finish by wrapping the weaving wire a few more times, trim it, and flatten/pinch down

the tail.

3. Shape the ring around your ring shaper or another object that's the right size. Try to secure it on tightly, because you'll need something to hold the ring steady as you finish the base wire ends.

4. This is another step where you can get creative. You'll have either four or six base wire ends coming from your weave, and to close your ring, you can make loops, spirals, twisted knots, and anything else you can think of. There are so many unique ways to finish this project, so let your imagination run wild!

That's it for the projects, but hopefully, these have inspired you to start creating your own designs. Play around with different weaves and stone sizes to make entirely new creations that are 100 percent your own.

[BONUS] Donut Bail Pendant

This is very simple work and thus requires simple skill. Because of its end product, which is a whole donut bail pendant, there will be a preparative work prior to the main job. In other words, this project is a beginner one but combines simple preparatory works with the main one. The preparation is expedient because without it the foundation will not be made for the huge job. In the same vein, the main job needs a pendant so, make sure the size and type of the pendant are determined too. Make sure you follow the steps swiftly even as you read.

The following are techniques needed to finish the job:

Weaving

Downhill single Flame Stitch

Wrapping

These techniques are very basic and must have been acquired from the beginning of this book if otherwise, make sure you revise the section that deals with techniques.

Materials:

33 in. 20-gauge dead-soft copper wire

3½ ft. 24-gauge dead-soft copper wire

50mm gemstone donut

10mm large-hole copper bead

3mm bead

40 80 seed beads

Daisy spacer with a large hole

Ruler

Chain nose pliers

Round nose pliers

The following are the things to get ready before going to the main work:

Step 1

Weave a bail for a donut-shaped stone with about a large 50mm jasper donut.

Step 2

Make sure that the weave is adjustable to fit any size

Step 3

Prepare the Downhill Single Flame Stitch technique for it would be needed at the woven section.

Step 4

You will need to learn if you have not mastered how to embellish with seed beads for a dash of color and texture.

To the main project now, make sure everything needed –the techniques, materials and the pre-working stages –is ready.

Then follow the step-by-step guide below:

Step 1

Making the base wire. For the base wire, pick a 20-gauge wire and cut six pieces of it. Drop this.

Step 2

Then, pick the 24-gauge wire and cut one piece of it for the weaving wire.

Step 3

At this stage, you will need to know how much wire needed for your base stone.

Step 4

Then, Wrap a cord or string through the stone.

Step 5

Make a mark for the overlap.

Step 6

Caution needs to be taken here make sure the measurement of this length is 2½ inches.

Step 7

To complete the overlapping, add 3 in. to that measurement of the length of the base wires.

Step 8

Make a cut of six 5½ in. pieces of wire.

Step 9

Pick up the base wire #6 at the top of the Weave.

Step 10

You will need to string a 60 seed bead about 1 in. from the end of base wire 6.

Step 11

Make sure that this spacer bead makes room in the weave to add more beads later.

Step 12

Pick the weaving wire, now, place it to the right of the bead and on top of the base wire. Make sure the placement is 1 in. from the end.

Step 13

Then, at the center where both wires (base and weaving) overlapped, hold it with your left thumb and index finger.

Step 14

With everything held in the right place and proportion, wrap the weaving wire three times to the right of the bead.

Step 15

You want to prepare the base wires for weaving. Do this by doing the Downhill Wire Preparation.

Step 16

For this Downhill wire preparation, make a

single Wrap.

Step 17

On base wire #1, at the bottom of the weave, string a spacer seed bead, and then complete the last wrap of the Downhill Wire Preparation.

Step 18

Remove the two spacer beads to the left and slide them back on base wires #1 and #6 to the right of the weave.

Step 19

Bring the weaving wire from behind up two base wires and go between base wires #4 and #5.

Step 20

Note that this must put you at the top of the hill as you bring the weaving wire up, over, and straight down the back, making the jump behind the weave so you can repeat the downhill pattern.

Step 21

Begin Downhill Flame Stitch Weave single wrap. At the bottom of every hill, at base wire #1, string a seed bead on base wires #1 and #6.

Step 22

You will continue with Downhill Flame Stitch Weave, stringing seed beads on base wires #1 and #6 as you go.

Step 23

Don't panic if your stitches don't want to stay in neat i.e., like in the diagonal lines because you could pinch them with chain nose pliers to make them line up.

Step 24

Now, continue the Downhill Flame Stitch Weave for the length you originally measured with the cord.

Step 25

When the weaving is completed, slide each wire out individually until the weave is centered.

Step 26

Then, wrap the weaving wire three times around base wire #6 and trim the end tightly on the back.

Step 27

You will need to push the weave into the hole of the stone and center the stone.

Step 28

With this, make a U-shaped bend to fit the stone very well. Now, remove the stone.

Step 29

You must have noticed that there are several ends that need to be finished.

Step 30

Because of this, make a 90-degree bend inward with base wires #1 and #6. They should cross each other inside the weave.

Step 31

At this stage, end base wires #2, #4, and #5 straight down on the inside of the weave, over the top of the two crossed wires. Make sure you trim all the three wires to about 3⁄8 in.

Step 32

With the round nose pliers, curl the ends of the three wires over the crossed wires to lock them in place.

Step 33

Trim the two crossed wires close, up against base wires #2 and #5.

Step 34

Repeat steps 9–11 on the other side of the

weave. Put the donut back in.

Step 35

Then, with chain nose pliers, pinch the two #3 base wires that are standing straight up.

Step 36

This will bring the two sides in, right up against each other for the next step.

Step 37

Make a double wrap around one of the #3 base wires. It doesn't matter which one, as long as it is tight.

Step 38

Trim the end and pinch it down.

Step 39

On the remaining base wire, string a spacer bead, a 10mm copper bead, and a 3mm bead.

Step 40

Make a Double-Wrapped Loop at the top of these beads. If you are adding a chain as you must have planned, connect the chain to the loop before you complete the wraps.

Your work is now ready. This is a very simple way of making stunning jewelry.

Making and Installing Clasps

When ending a piece of jewelry, most notably, bracelet, necklace, etc., the clasp is what hold the two ends together. A clasp connects both ends of the piece, allowing you to open and close the piece when putting it on or taking it off while complimenting its beauty. There are quite a number of clasps designs, and this is also subject to creativity and innovation. Many types of clasps are available in the market for purchase, but you make yours. To mention but a few, we have the loop clasps, S-clasp, etc.

In this book, we will be considering how to make a few clasps and also how to install them.

1. S-Clasp

Materials:

Wire- two pieces of 20 gauge wire of 3cm each

Round nose pliers

Mandrel- pen (this is optional)

Steps

d. Measure and cut the stipulated amount of wire. Mark, using a marker, the 1/3 point of the wire both from ends and using a round nose plier, make a curve in the wire at each of this point to form an S shape.

e. With the tip of your round nose plier, make small loops at each ends facing outwards.

f. Now close one side tightly though cautiously. The open side serves as the clasps.

NOTE: To install this S-Clasp on a bracelet or necklace. Attach one side to one loop of the bracelet before closing it tightly. The other side will be left open, and this side gives ease of wearing.

2. The loop clasp

Materials:

Round nose plier

Wire of 5 or 6.”

Steps

n. Pick the wire of 5 or 6" and use the round nose plier to bend one of the ends of the wire over to about 1.5" from the end

o. Then, make a loop by wrapping the wire ends around the pliers.

p. Then, to finish the wrapping process, hold the bottom of the pliers and complete it.

q. While making the loop, be very sure that the whole is very large to contain the hook you want to use.

r. Turn and bring the wire around and keep rolling the wire in order to make the loop center over the wire.

s. Hold the loop very well with the pliers and wrap the wire up to two to three times.

t. When the loop is fine in shape, clip close

it.

u. Peradventure, the wraps are not close together and take the bent nose pliers and pinch everything up.

v. Turn the clipped end to face you, grab and hold the wire above the wrap.

w. After the grab at length, bend it towards the back

x. At this point, you will need to make the loop like the time you started. Wrap down the first wrap.

y. Now you will need to make a clip very close to the first wrap that you've bent.

z. Then, squeeze smoothly so that the ends of the clip will join together.

This is the end of your clasp. Mind you, there are many things that can be attached to this clasp. In fact, earrings can fit in very well.

Chapter 3: Personalizing Projects

The only downside to using patterns is that they're not unique or personalized if you follow them to the letter. However, as you've just seen in the projects from the previous chapter, there are endless ways you can alter a pattern or add something to it to add your own touch of creativity. Here are some ways you can personalize cookie-cutter projects without getting too complicated:

Use a Different Weave Technique

As an intermediate weaver, you now have a good number of techniques under your belt. These techniques can be modified and adapted to suit any project you're working on. Many more advanced weavers even make up their own designs as they go. Don't ever feel restricted by the weave that's suggested. If it's purely for aesthetic reasons and isn't vital to the structural integrity of the piece, change away.

Add Beads/Change the Bead Size or Style

A few of the projects in Chapter 2 either included beads or mentioned that beads could be added. You can do this with nearly any project. If the project already calls for the use of beads, you don't have to use the same size or style bead as the instructions say. Use a smaller or larger center stone, add faceted beads instead of round, and make your pieces stand out even more by including beads where the pattern does not. Just make sure you first read through the instructions thoroughly to ensure any alterations you make won't affect a later aspect of the design.

Get Creative with Your Supplies

You may not always have all the materials on

hand that you need for a project. Instead of rushing out to the nearest crafting store, see if you can make do with what you have on hand. Who knows, you may end up making something you like better than you first thought you would.

Also, remember that even if a certain wire material is specified, you don't necessarily have to use that kind. If you want to use copper instead of silver or silver instead of brass (and so on and so forth), that's up to you. It is recommended that you stick with the wire hardness that the pattern suggests, though, since that will directly affect the ease with which you can weave as well as the structure of the end result.

Chapter 4: Common Wire Weaving Problems

No art form is without its own unique difficulties. Wire weaving, in particular, poses a few challenges for beginners and experts alike. You don't have to stress about it, though. Others have come before you and paved the way so that your own journey would be easier.

Here are five of the most common problems or questions you might encounter while wire weaving and how to solve them.

What Are Some Inexpensive but Effective Wire Choices for First Timers/Intermediate Weavers?

Perhaps the most important decision you'll make about any project is the type of wire you use. Your wire choice defines the look and ease of the project, so it's best to be informed about all your options and have a few tried and tested options that you regularly turn to.

A surprising discovery made by many people just getting into wire weaving is that there are more wire options than expected. Some of the most common metals used in jewelry making are copper, aluminum, nickel, brass, sterling silver, and iron. Many metals can be made in different colors like the traditional gold and silver using filling and plating processes.

For beginner and intermediate weavers alike, copper is often the ideal choice. It's inexpensive and easy to work with, plus it makes beautiful designs and is readily available in a wide range of gauges.

Another option is pure or fine silver wire. It's less prone to breaking than sterling silver and thus is much easier (and less frustrating) to work with.

How Do I Stop Overworking and Mangling My Base Wires?

Your base wires are the framework of your weaving project and will either make your life easier or cause you endless headaches. Handling them takes practice, but there are a few things you can do to speed up the learning process.

1. Be sure you cut the right length for your project. Too short, and you'll be struggling to weave too much wire on limited space; too long, and you'll have extra wire tripping you up and making you fumble around. Both scenarios lead to mangled base wires as you try to work around the lack or excess.

2. Relax your grip. When we're working with small tools and tiny wires, we have a tendency to tense up and hold our base wires like they're slippery eels. Switch to a firm but gentle grip that won't leave

your hand tired and your wires bent out of shape.

3. Use the right gauge base wires. Most projects will call for 18 gauge, because this is an easy size to work with, and you can create many different weave patterns using it. If your base wires feel flimsy or soft, double check the gauge. Your problem could be as simple as mislabeled packaging or an unintentional switch.

How Can I Make Wire Weaving Easier on My Hands?

Jewelry making is a hands-on business. Your poor palms and chapped fingers will be begging for a break before too long if they haven't already; however, your solution doesn't have to be to stop and step away from the crafting table for a few days. On the contrary, if you stop working with your projects for too long, not only will you lose motivation, but you'll also find that it hurts more when you come back to it. Just as guitar players develop calluses from their guitar strings, you will develop jewelry maker calluses; wear them proudly.

Of course, you don't have to accept the pain. One option you can use if you want to avoid calluses or have painful ones already is to wrap your fingers in medical tape or bandages to prevent the wire from rubbing against your skin. You can also use lotion to soothe and soften your hands.

Aside from calluses, cramping and carpal tunnel are also problems that could develop when you work with thin wires and perform repetitive motions. One way to counter this is to take frequent breaks while you're working on a project to let your hands rest and try not to hold the wires in a vice grip. You can also perform hand and finger strengthening exercises - the rest of your body gets stronger when you work out, so why shouldn't your extremities?

Is There a Way to Oxidize Metal Without Liver of Sulfur?

If you don't already know, liver of sulfur is used to give an antique look to jewelry by oxidizing it, which means the metal is chemically combined with oxygen. It reacts with the metal in a way that causes it to take on a darkened appearance. What if you don't want to use chemicals, though? What if the smell of liver of sulfur makes you sick? It's not the most pleasant smell, after all.

There are other ways to oxidize metals. Here are a few:

1. You can use boiled eggs, surprisingly enough. Yes, it does sound disgusting, and no, this probably wouldn't be your first choice, but if you're ever in a pinch or want a cheaper way to add patina, boil a couple of eggs, crush them up in a bag with the shells, and let the metals you want oxidized sit in the bag with the

mixture for as long as it takes to darken them to the stage you want.

2. You can also soak the metal in white vinegar along with hydrogen peroxide and salt, though in some cases hydrogen peroxide alone might be enough.

How and Where Can I Substitute Silver Wire with Copper Wire?

When you're learning a new weave or trying a new design for the first time, you'll more than likely choose copper as your material. However, when you're looking to gift your creations or even sell them, when is copper okay and when should silver be your first choice?

One big issue with copper is that if it oxidizes or you do it yourself to create an antique look, the patina or tarnish can rub off onto the skin of the wearer. This gives skin a green tinge, which can be disconcerting.

If you want to use copper wire in place of silver, keep in mind who will be wearing it, what part of the body the piece will be on, and if the majority of the piece is made from copper or just some of it. If you're making wire woven earrings, for example, the only part you need to worry about coming into contact with the skin is the ear wire. If the earring is copper but the wire is something like stainless steel, you should have no problem.

Chapter 5: How to Make Your Own Findings

Wire is good for more than just weaving! You can also use it to make your own findings. This not only saves money, but it allows you to make your designs even more unique. Wouldn't you like to be able to say your piece is 100 percent handmade, findings and all? While there are some findings you will want to buy just because they're intricate or difficult to make, there's no reason you can't start making the following right away.

Jump Rings

Jump rings are essential in various designs. While you can buy them from any craft store, why bother if you already have oodles of wire around?

The size of your jump rings and the gauge of wire you use will vary depending on the project, but to try your hand at it to see if you prefer making your own, follow these steps:

1. Using 18 gauge round copper wire, make coils with either a Coiling Gizmo (using a thicker rod) or by wrapping the wire around something round that's the correct thickness for the rings you're making.

2. Using wire cutters, trim the ends of your coil so that they're even with the rest of the coil and aren't sticking out at odd angles. You want the cuts to be smooth, because if you look at most jump rings, the open ends are both flat so they can fit together easily.

3. Loosen the whole coil, then take your wire cutters and cut your first ring at the second coil in the spot where the end of the first coil is. This makes more sense once you have the coil in front of you. It's fairly simple to know where to cut to

make the proper jump ring shape.

4. Cut all the coils in the same manner, and there you have it. You've made your own jump rings and can now experiment with different gauges and sizes.

Hook Clasps

Many handmade bracelets close with a hook clasp. Oftentimes, though, you can only get these in sets of two or three, and they're way more expensive than they should be. Both of those problems go away if you make your own.

1. Using 16 gauge round dead soft wire, cut about 2.75 inches off and use a jewelry file to smooth down both ends nicely.

2. Make a loop on one end of the wire using round nose pliers. Try to make the loop as wide as the widest part of your pliers.

3. At the other end of the wire, take about a quarter of an inch of the wire and bend it

up at a 90-degree angle in the opposite direction of your curled loop.

4. Find the center of the wire between the loop and the 90-degree angle. Using your pliers, bend that the same direction you bent the angle to form a rectangle that has about a quarter-inch opening between the bent angle and the straight part of the wire. The rectangle and the loop should be on the opposite side.

This is a fairly simple hook clasp. Feel free to play around with it to come up with different methods and designs.

Ear Wires

There are so many different types of ear wires, but a few of the most popular are lever backs, french hooks, and kidney wires. All you need to make your own are pliers and a few inches of 20 gauge wire in the metal you like best. Keep in mind that copper can cause discoloration, so you may want to stick with sterling silver.

All you really need to do is bend the wire into the proper shape, which you can do by looking online to find a shape you like; you can also use a pair of your own earrings as a reference.

Which Pieces You Should Still Buy

As mentioned previously, there are some findings that take more work than they're worth, including the following:

- Crimps

- Pin backs

- Bead tips

- Crimp covers

- Bead caps

Thankfully, all of these supplies are relatively cheap and easy to find.

Chapter 6: Cold Connections

You know the image of the burly blacksmith hammering away at metals heated to astonishing temperatures and forging massive swords fit for warriors? It turns out that that's not the only way to connect two or more pieces of metal. While metalsmithing and forging are exciting hobbies, they're a little too much work for someone who's just getting into the art of jewelry making. If you're new to working with metals or don't have a lot of experience crafting, take your time to learn the processes that come before the more labor-intensive techniques.

To join pieces of metal, you can either use warm connections, such as soldering and welding, or you can use cold connections. We're going to focus on cold connections, but don't let the name fool you. Just because these methods don't involve heat doesn't mean that they aren't effective and durable.

There are two different types of cold connections: pierced and adhered. Both types incorporate a few different techniques which are explained in more detail below. One isn't necessarily better than the other. It all depends on the project you're working on, the tools available to you, and the look you want the finished product to have. Before you can decide, however, you need to know what each entails.

Pierced Cold Connections

Despite the name, pierced cold connections do not necessarily have to be pierced. There are two main techniques: riveting and wireworking. You should be very familiar with wireworking by now, because wire weaving is a type of wireworking. There are a few others that are discussed below, but first, we'll look at the different rivets and how to use them.

Riveting

Riveting may sound like a complicated process, but it's actually straightforward. If the piece you're working with already has holes or you plan to add holes, rivets are probably going to be your best bet. There are many different types of rivets including eyelets, semi-tubular, and nail-head, and they're separated into two categories: open rivets and solid rivets. The rivet you choose will depend on your project and personal preference. Open rivets typically feature a tube that allows for the use of jump rings and other connectors or wire, while solid rivets don't.

The tools you need may vary depending on the type of rivet you use, but in general, you will need the following:

- Riveting hammer

- File and/or wire cutters

- Bench block

- Drill set

If you don't want to purchase and try out a bunch of different rivets to decide which you like best, you can always go old school and use wire to make wire rivets. Since you're already learning wire weaving and are familiar with the various gauges and metals, this might be the best option to start out with, although it's a bit more labor-intensive. For this method, you'll need the tools listed above, plus the metals you want to join, along with wire that fits into the holes you already have drilled or intend to drill. The wire should fit snugly; this will be a solid rivet. Detailed instructions on how to make wire rivets can be found online, but here's a quick run-through:

1. Cut enough wire so that 0.5 to 1mm will be left on either side of the joined metal.

2. Make sure that your wire fits the holes that you have drilled in your metal pieces and that the ends of the wire are flat and

smoothed out. If they're uneven, your rivet will be messy and could have sharp edges.

3. Set the metal with the inserted wire on your bench block (steel is best). Using your riveting hammer, tap on the top of the wire on one side, then flip the piece over and do the same on the other side. You're trying to sandwich the metal between the flattened tops of the wire, so you'll probably have to repeat this process a few times to ensure the metals are tight together and that the wire is smooth and domed on either side.

It's as easy as that. Of course, the first few times you try this, it won't be so simple. Start out with cheap materials that you can practice with until you get your technique down. Alternatively, you can use nail-head rivets, which come with one side pre-hammered so that all you have to do is tap down the other side instead of both sides - but where's the fun in that?

Wireworking

As already mentioned, wire weaving is a type of wireworking because it involves the use of wire to create a solid item. Other methods of wireworking include wire wrapping and wire stitching. Since you're already familiar with wire weaving, we're going to take a closer look at the other two.

Wire wrapping is a very popular technique that is often used with stones to make beautiful and unique necklaces and earrings. It's similar to wire weaving, except it doesn't make use of base wires and typically involves a focal piece such as a gemstone or pendant. Basic wire wrapping starts with a frame that goes around the edges of the center stone being wrapped. To make the frame, you'll usually need the following items:

- 20 gauge square soft wire

- 22 gauge half-round hard wire

- Wire cutters

- Flat nose pliers

- Tape

- Felt tip pen

- Ruler

While some steps may vary from project to project, here is how a basic frame is made:

1. Cut six pieces of the 20 gauge wire measuring about 8 inches (though the length may vary depending on the center stone size). These are your main frame wires that will go around the perimeter of the stone.

2. Line up the six pieces side by side and tape them together at the ends. You want them all to be as even as possible, since in the next step you'll be binding them to create a solid frame.

3. Use your felt tip pen to draw a line through the center of the frame (this will

be at about 4 inches). The line represents your first binding site.

4. Cut a 5-inch piece of the 22 gauge wire. This is your binding wire.

5. Wrap the binding wire around the center mark you made on the frame using your flat nose pliers. There should be equal lengths of binding on either side of the mark, and the wraps should be snug up against one another so no gaps show.

6. Measure out a quarter-inch from the edge of the binding on either side and then another quarter-inch from each of those lines. In between the two lines you just drew on either side of the middle binding, you're going to repeat step 5. You should have a total of three bindings wrapped around the frame.

The steps can vary greatly from this point, but this should provide you with a place to start. From here, you can add your stone and let your imagination run wild as you design intricate loops and curls around the centerpiece and along the frame. There are endless ways to go from here, so play around with it and see what you can create.

Wire stitching is a lot more complex and is beyond the scope of this book, but there are many resources out there if you want to give it a try. It essentially involves joining rows of beads using stitch-like patterns, but with wire instead of thread.

Adhered Cold Connections

The name alone is fairly self-explanatory. Adhered cold connections make use of bonding materials to hold pieces of metal together. Don't underestimate the power of adhesion; jewelry-grade materials are made to be durable and stick to smaller surface areas. It's like soldering, only without heat. The two most common bonding materials used by jewelers are glue and clay.

Glue

This isn't your typical Elmer's glue that kids use to make macaroni art. Jewelry glue is tough, but it also allows you to create professional quality pieces because it's designed not to look tacky. With the right application techniques, no one will even be able to tell it's there.

Some tips for applying jeweler's glue include the following:

- Prepare your metal surfaces by sanding them so the glue has something to hold onto.

- A little goes a long way. Start off with less than you think you'll need and add more from there.

- Most glues need time to set, so ensure you have some sort of clamping mechanism to avoid having to manually hold the pieces together until you're sure they've adhered.

The three most popular (and effective) jewelry glue includes E-6000, Gorilla Glue, and Devcon Epoxy. E-6000 is thick and flexible, and it's useful in that it doesn't dry immediately, meaning you can make adjustments after applying it so that it sets in just the way you want it to. Gorilla Glue takes several hours to dry and should only be used when you need an extra strong connection. Devcon Epoxy can be found in both 2 -minute and 30-minute set time formulas, but be careful with either one, because the materials will generally bind right away and will be more difficult to adjust than those with E-6000.

Clay

While there's no decorative element provided by glue, clay, on the other hand, can be used to not only create a cold connection, but also enhance the visual appeal of a piece. It can be especially effective if you're working with delicate metals with a very small surface area that is too difficult to glue. Kato Polyclay and Vitrium Clay are the standard choices, and both offer color options that expand the possibilities depending on how unique your pieces are. Vitrium Clay is also available translucent if you want to keep things simple.

One thing to keep in mind is that while Vitrium will air dry, Kato Polyclay needs to be baked in order to cure, so it's not a purely cold method of connection. On the plus side, you can use it for more than just adhering metals. There's a big market for handcrafted beads, and with polyclays, you can come up with your own designs.

Chapter 7: Suppliers and Resources

Nothing in this book would be possible without the right supplies and resources. If you're at an intermediate stage, you probably already have a cache of supplies, but it doesn't hurt to know where to shop in the future. It's an unfortunate truth that many local craft stores are far too expensive to sustain a hobby, and that's where online retailers come in. A few standout options have made a name for themselves in the jewelry-making world. If you don't already know about them, below we have detailed some places you should look into.

Rio Grande

If you talk to any wire weaver about where they get their supplies, they'll more than likely start waxing poetic about Rio Grande. Based out of New Mexico, Rio Grande offers chains, findings, packaging, organizers, tools, metals, and practically anything else you could possibly need to start any craft you wish. They've become dependable for their excellent prices and quality supplies.

MonsterSlayer

Also based out of New Mexico, MonsterSlayer has an incredibly vast inventory of not just wire, but every kind of jewelry supply need out there. Their website isn't the most user-friendly, but if you need an obscure metal or are looking for some really unique items, you should definitely take a look on MonsterSlayer's site.

Alibaba

You can't be in the jewelry world and not know about Alibaba. They offer bulk goods in every category, including jewelry supplies. The shipping times are a bit long (sometimes over a month), but the quality is surprisingly good and the prices are phenomenal. If you want a lot of supplies for the price of a few, Alibaba is your best bet.

Etsy

While Etsy is marketed as the place to find handmade goods, it also has excellent supply stores. Sure, the prices aren't the lowest, but if you need something fast or are looking for supplies that might not be sold elsewhere, it's worth looking on Etsy. Besides, if you one day decide you want to sell your wire woven creations, it helps to know the system and establish a relationship with a trusted supplier.

Leave a Review?

Throughout the process of writing this book, I have tried to put down as much value and knowledge for the reader as possible. Some things I knew some others I spent the time to research. I hope you found this book to be of benefit to you.

If you liked the book, would you consider leaving a review for it? It would really help my book, and I would be grateful to you for letting other people know that you like it.

Yours Sincerely,

Amy Lange

Conclusion

Congratulations on getting to the end of *Intermediate Wire Weaving*! By now, you've learned a few new weaves, put those weaves to the test with some fun projects, discovered how to personalize future projects, and gained some knowledge about other jewelry making techniques that will help you make even more amazing creations in the future.

Don't worry if it didn't all make sense on the first go. Even though you're past the beginner stages, there's still a lot to learn, and it does get more difficult from here. Never give up, though. Above all else, wire weaving is supposed to be fun. If you're pressuring yourself to make perfect designs the first time, learn a new weave as fast as possible, or if you are generally turning the process into a chore, you'll lose interest before long. The best way to avoid this is to leave perfection out of the equation. Mistakes often lead to innovation, so don't be afraid to make a few; they might just turn into your best pieces.

From here, keep practicing the weaves from Chapter 1, and add some personalized touches to the projects in Chapter 2. There's a world of possibilities open to you now, so set out those wires, get some stones ready, roll up your sleeves, and just weave!

Resources

Anderson, J. (2010, June 08). Woven Wire Ring Tutorial. Retrieved from https://www.youtube.com/watch?v=iQ-Az7jIeFA

Klingenberg, R. (n.d.). Easy Wire Hook Clasp (Tutorial). Retrieved from https://jewelrymakingjournal.com/easy-wire-hook-clasp-tutorial/

Knaus, T. (n.d.). Wire-woven brooch. Retrieved from http://www.facetjewelry.com/metal-wire/projects/2016/05/wire-woven-brooch

Making an Ear Wire. (n.d.). Retrieved from https://www.fusionbeads.com/making-an-ear-wire

OxanaCrafts. (2016, July 02). Framed Tree Of Life Cabochon Pendant Wire Wrap Tutorial. Retrieved from

https://www.youtube.com/watch?v=gfJPosJW
ikw

OxanaCrafts. (2016, May 20). Wire Wrap
Tutorial Filigree Crystal Earrings. Retrieved
from
https://www.youtube.com/watch?v=hindW3I
SnfU

OxanaCrafts. (2016, July 01). Wire Wrapped
Coiled Pendant Tutorial (Cabochon). Retrieved
from
https://www.youtube.com/watch?v=APb48z6
c9do

Van Look, B. (n.d.). Jewelry-Making Articles.
Retrieved from
https://www.firemountaingems.com/resource
s/jewelry-making-articles/c12a

Metric Conversion Chart

Length Conversion Table of Common Length Units

	Milli meter (mm)	Centi mete r (cm)	Mete r (m)	Kilo meter (km)	Inch (in)	Foot/ feet (ft)	Yard (yd)
1 mill ime ter (m m)	1	0.1	0.001	0.00 0001	0.3937 00787 40157	0.00 3280 8398 9501 31	0.00 1093 6132 9833 77
1 cent ime ter (cm)	10	1	0.01	0.00 001	0.3937 00787 40157	0.03 2808 3989 50131	0.01 093 6132 9833 77
1 met er (m)	1000	100	1	0.001	39.370 07874 0157	3.280 8398 9501 31	1.09 3613 2983 377
1 kilo met er (km)	1000 000	1000 00	1000	1	39370. 07874 0157	3280. 8398 9501 31	1093 .613 2983 377
1 inch (in)	25.4	2.54	0.025 4	0.00 0025 4	1	0.08 3333 3333	0.02 7777 7777

							33333	77778
1 foot / feet (ft)	304.8	30.48	0.3048	0.00003048	12	1	0.333333333333
1 yard (yd)	914.4	91.44	0.9144	0.00009144	36	3	1

Wire conversion Chart

Gauge	Inches	Millimeters
10	0.102	2.59
11	0.091	2.31
12	0.081	2.06
13	0.072	1.83
14	0.064	1.63
15	0.057	1.45
16	0.052	1.29
17	0.0045	1.14
18	0.04	1.02
19	0.0036	0.91
20	0.032	0.81

21	0.028	0.71
22	0.025	0.64
23	0.023	0.58
24	0.02	0.51
25	0.0179	0.455
26	0.0159	0.404
27	0.0142	0.361
28	0.0126	0.32
29	0.0113	0.287
30	0.01	0.25
31	0.0089	0.226
32	0.008	0.2
33	0.0071	0.18
34	0.0063	0.16
35	0.0056	0.142
36	0.005	0.13
37	0.0045	0.114
38	0.004	0.1

The conversation given here is strictly on the measurement used throughout the book. Apply your calculation using a calculator where necessary. Note that while measuring the wires, the centimeter and millimeter gauge of the wire could be used too with a ruler.